BUDDHISM

ITS HISTORY AND LITERATURE

AMERICAN LECTURES ON THE HISTORY OF RELIGIONS
FIRST SERIES—1894-1895

BUDDHISM

ITS HISTORY AND LITERATURE

BY

T. W. RHYS DAVIDS, LL.D., PH.D.

Chairman of the Pali Text Society, Secretary and Librarian of the Royal Asiatic Society, Professor of Pali and Buddhist Literature at University College, London

SECOND EDITION

GYAN

Published by

GYAN

Gyan Publishing House
5, Ansari Road
Daryaganj, New Delhi-110002
Phone: 011-47034999, 9811692060
E-mail: books@gyanbooks.com

Distribution Network
gyanbooks.com
India, USA, Canada, UK, Australia, France

ISBN : 978-81-212-2194-8 (PB)
First Published, 1907

2nd Impression 2021

Printed at: Gyan Press, Delhi.

Buddhism its History and Literature
Author: T. W. Rhys Davids

AMERICAN LECTURES ON THE HISTORY OF RELIGIONS

FIRST SERIES—1894-1895

BUDDHISM

ITS HISTORY AND LITERATURE

BY

T. W. RHYS DAVIDS, LL.D., PH.D.

Chairman of the Pali Text Society, Secretary and Librarian of the Royal Asiatic Society, Professor of Pali and Buddhist Literature at University College, London

SECOND EDITION

G. P. PUTNAM'S SONS

NEW YORK
27 WEST TWENTY-THIRD STREET

LONDON
24 BEDFORD STREET, STRAND

The Knickerbocker Press

1907

ANNOUNCEMENT.

ON the 24th of December, 1891, fifteen persons interested in promoting the historical study of religions united in issuing a circular-letter inviting a conference in the Council Chambers of the Historical Society of Philadelphia, on the 30th of the same month, for the purpose of instituting "popular courses in the History of Religions, somewhat after the style of the Hibbert lectures in England, to be delivered annually by the best scholars of Europe and this country, in various cities, such as Baltimore, Boston, Brooklyn, Chicago, New York, Philadelphia, and others." There participated in this conference personally or by letter, from Philadelphia, Rev. Prof. E. T. Bartlett, D.D., Rev. George Dana Boardman, D.D., Prof. D. G. Brinton, M.D., Sc.D., Horace Howard Furness, LL.D., Prof. E. J. James, Ph.D., Prof. Morris Jastrow, Jr., Ph.D., Provost Wm. Pepper, M.D. LL.D., of the University of Pennsylvania, Hon. Mayer Sulzberger, Mrs. Cornelius Stevenson, and Talcott Williams, LL.D.; from Baltimore, Prest. D. C. Gilman, LL.D., of the Johns Hopkins University, and Prof. Paul Haupt, Ph.D.; from Boston and Cambridge, Rev. E. E. Hale, D.D., Prof. C. R. Lanman, Ph.D., Prof. D. G. Lyon, Ph.D., and Prof. C. H. Toy, LL.D.; from Brooklyn, Rev. Edward F. Braislin, D.D., and Prof. Franklin W. Hooper, of the Brooklyn Institute; from Chicago, Pres. W. R. Harper, Ph.D., of the University of Chicago, and Rev. Prof. Emil G. Hirsch, Ph.D.; from New York, Rev. Prof. C. A. Briggs, D.D., LL.D., Rev. Prof. Francis Brown, D.D., Rev. G. Gottheil, D.D., Prof. R. J. H. Gottheil, Ph.D., Rev. John P. Peters, Ph.D., Sc.D., D.D., and Rev. W. Hayes Ward, D.D., LL.D.; from Ithaca, N. Y., Pres. J. G. Schurman, of Cornell University, and Hon. Andrew D. White, LL.D.

At this conference, Prof. Jastrow submitted a plan for establishing popular lecture courses on the historical study of religions by securing the co-operation of existing institutions and lecture associations, such as the Lowell, Brooklyn, and Peabody Institutes, the University Lecture Association of Philadelphia, and some of our colleges and universities. Each course, according to this plan, was to consist of from six to eight lectures, and the engagement of lecturers, choice of subjects, and so forth were to be in the hands of a committee chosen from the different cities, and representing the various institutions and associations participating.

This general scheme met with the cordial approval of the conference, which voted the project both a timely and useful one, and which appointed Dean Bartlett, Prof. Jastrow, and Dr. Peters a committee to elaborate a plan of organisation and report at an adjourned meeting. That meeting was held at the Union Theological Seminary in New York City, February 6, 1892, and, as a result, an association was organised for the purpose of encouraging the study of religions. The *terms* of association then adopted, with slight modifications introduced later, are as follows:

1.—The object of this Association shall be to provide courses of lectures on the history of religions, to be delivered in various cities.

2.—The Association shall be composed of delegates from institutions agreeing to co-operate, or from local boards, organised where such co-operation is not possible.

3.—These Delegates—one from each Institution or Local Board, shall constitute themselves a Council under the name of the "American Committee for Lectures on the History of Religions."

4.—The Council shall elect out of its number a President, a Secretary, and a Treasurer.

5.—All matters of local detail shall be left to the

Institutions or Local Boards, under whose auspices the lectures are to be delivered.

6.—A course of lectures on some religion, or phase of religion, from an historical point of view, or on a subject germane to the study of religions, shall be delivered annually, or at such intervals as may be found practicable, in the different cities represented by this Association.

7.—The Council (*a*) shall be charged with the selection of the lecturers, (*b*) shall have charge of the funds, (*c*) shall assign the time for the lectures in each city, and perform such other functions as may be necessary.

8.—Polemical subjects, as well as polemics in the treatment of subjects, shall be positively excluded.

9.—The lecturer shall be chosen by the Council, at least ten months before the date fixed for the course of lectures.

10.—The lectures shall be delivered in the various cities between the months of October and June.

11.—The Copyright of the lectures shall be the property of the Association.

12.—One half of the lecturer's compensation shall be paid at the completion of his entire course, and the second half upon the publication of the lectures.

13.—The compensation offered to the lecturer shall be fixed in each case by the Council.

14.—The lecturer is not to deliver elsewhere any of the lectures for which he is engaged by the Committee, except with the sanction of the Committee.

The Committee appointed to carry out this plan and the institutions represented are:

Prof. C. H. Toy, LL.D., of Harvard University, representing Boston and Cambridge, President.

Prest. J. G. Schurman, representing Cornell University.

Prof. Franklin W. Hooper, representing the Brooklyn Institute.

Prof. J. F. Jameson, representing the Brown University Lecture Association (joined the Association in 1894).

Prof. Paul Haupt, Ph.D., of Johns Hopkins University, representing the Peabody Institute.

Prof. Morris Jastrow, Jr., Ph.D., of the University of Pennsylvania, representing the University Lecture Association, Secretary.

Prof. R. J. H. Gottheil, Ph.D., of Columbia College,

and Rev. John P. Peters, Ph.D., Treasurer, representing the New York lecture committee.

For its first course, the Committee selected as the lecturer Prof. T. W. Rhys Davids, Ph.D., LL.D., of London, England, and as the subject, "The History and Literature of Buddhism." Prof. Davids is well known to all who are interested in the study of Indian religions. Few writers have contributed so much to our knowledge of Buddhism as he. In 1878 he wrote for the London Society for the Promotion of Christian Knowledge, a sketch of the life of Gotama the Buddha, which was published under the title *Buddhism*. In 1881 he delivered the Hibbert Lectures, his subject being "The Origin and Growth of Religion as Illustrated by Some Points in the History of Indian Buddhism." In conjunction with Prof. H. Oldenberg, he published in the *Sacred Books of the East* translations of *Vinaya Texts*. The long list of his works includes *Questions of King Milinda*, *Buddhist Birth Stories*, *The Ancient Coins and Measures of Ceylon*, *The Description of Sigiri the Lion Rock*, besides many other publications. Prof. Davids is also secretary of the Pali Text Society, and a constant contributor to its publications.

Prof. Davids' course, consisting of six lectures, was delivered before large audiences during the winter of

1894–1895 at Cornell University, Ithaca, N. Y.; Lowell Institute, Boston; Brown University, Providence; Brooklyn Institute, Brooklyn; Columbia College, New York; and a course comprising four of these lectures was delivered at the Peabody Institute, Baltimore, and the University of Pennsylvania, Philadelphia. It is these lectures that are now presented to the public in book form.

The object of this Association is to provide the best opportunities for bringing to the knowledge of the public at large the methods and results of those distinguished specialists who have devoted their lives to the study of the religions of other countries and other ages. It is safe to say that there is no other subject of modern research which concerns all classes so nearly as the study of religions. This course of lectures is the first fruit of the Association's labours, and it is offered to the public in the full assurance that it will so commend itself to all thoughtful readers as to win approval of the large work which the Association has undertaken. It is the hope of the Committee to provide courses of lectures at intervals of two years, or oftener, if the encouragement which the undertaking receives warrants it, and the practical difficulties involved in securing competent lecturers do not make it impossible.

Arrangements have so far been completed for two further courses of lectures, one by Prof. D. G. Brinton, M.D., Sc.D., of the University of Pennsylvania, on "The Religions of Primitive Peoples," to be delivered during the coming winter, 1896–97; and one by the Rev. Prof. T. K. Cheyne, M.A., D.D., Canon of Rochester, on "Religious Thought and Life among the Ancient Hebrews," to be delivered during the winter of 1897–98.

JOHN P. PETERS,
C. H. TOY,
MORRIS JASTROW, JR., } *Committee on Publication.*

March 29, 1896.

TABLE OF CONTENTS.

LECTURE I. RELIGIOUS THEORIES IN INDIA BEFORE BUDDHISM.

	PAGE
Religion, the meaning of the word	1
Value, from the comparative point of view, of the history of the Buddhist religion	6
Theories of God and the Soul, generally	10
The same in India; the Vedas	14
Rise of monotheism, especially in India	19
The Lokāyatas and Jains	24
The Sānkhya system	24
The Sixty-two Heresies	30
Summary of this chapter	36
Importance attached by Buddhist writers to the question of the soul-theory	39

LECTURE II. AUTHORITIES ON WHICH OUR KNOWLEDGE OF BUDDHISM IS BASED.

Interest of the discovery of new literatures	44, 45
First discovery of Pali	46
Turnour's Mahā Vansa	47
Prof. Fausböll's Dhammapada	48
The Dictionary	49
The Three Piṭakas	52
The Vinaya, Rules of the Order	54
The Great Nikāyas	58
The Abhidhamma	62
The miscellaneous books	65
Quotations from the Songs of the Sisters	73–75
The Pali Text Society	80–86
List of the Piṭakas	83

LECTURE III. NOTES ON THE LIFE OF THE BUDDHA.

PAGE

No ancient biography extant 87
The Pali and Sanskrit poems 88
The Sākya clan 91
The Buddha not a king's son 92
The legends of his birth and childhood 93
The Great Renunciation 96
King Bimbisāra's offer 99
The Teachers 102
Attainment of Nirvana 104
First Sermon 105
Daily life 108
The Buddha and the Brahmins 113

LECTURE IV. THE SECRET OF BUDDHISM.

PART I. THE SIGNS, THE PATH, AND THE FETTERS.

The Ajanta cave fresco of the Wheel 118
Wonders of the Wheel 120
Impermanence 123
Sorrow and individuality 124
Delusions about self or soul 125
Karma 129
Future life 131
The Noble Eightfold Path 135
The Four Noble Truths 136
Modern parallels 140
The Ten Fetters 141
Nirvana 151

LECTURE V. THE SECRET OF BUDDHISM.

PART II. THE WHEEL OF LIFE AND ARAHATSHIP (OR NIRVANA).

Salvation, from what? 153
The Twelve Causes 155
Grasping the cause of rebirth 159
Western parallels 160

PAGE
Nirvana 162
Poems on 166
The bliss of 171
The longing for it 172
Where it can be got 175
The ideal Recluse 176
Intellectual activity part of ideal Arahatship 181
Suppression of desire not a part of it 182
The Freedom in Arahatship 184
Real basis of the importance of the study of this ideal . . 186

LECTURE VI. SOME NOTES ON THE HISTORY OF BUDDHISM.

The various Buddhisms 187
Council of Vesāli 190
Kathā Vatthu 195
The seventeen schools 197
Bodhisatship 199
The Greater Vehicle 204
The Tantra books 207
Theosophy 209
Schopenhauer and Huxley on Buddhism 220

INDEX 223

BUDDHISM.

LECTURE I.

Religious Theories in India before Buddhism.

IT has often been maintained that there is no nation or tribe without religion. But what is meant by religion? The word, as is well known, is not found in languages not related to our own, and its derivation is uncertain. Cicero, in one passage, derived it from *re* and *lego*, and held that its real meaning was the repetition of prayers and incantations. Another interpretation derives the word from *re* and *ligo*, and makes its original sense that of attachment, of a continual binding (that is, no doubt, to the gods). A third derivation connects the word with *lex*, and explains it as a law-abiding, scrupulously conscientious, frame of mind. This last seems to be most in accordance with the conceptions prevalent when the use of the phrase began, and more in harmony with the similar expressions that arose under similar circumstances elsewhere—in China, for instance, and in India. In India, indeed, the same word is used by the followers of every school of thought for law and for religion—the word Dharma, etymologically equivalent to the Latin *forma*, and constantly reminding us in its implied connotation of the English phrase "good form."

Law did not, of course, in that early time, mean legislation. It was rather custom, established precedent; and a sense of duty to the established order of things included and implied a reverential attitude toward the gods. This last side of the idea tended, even in Roman usage, to become predominant; and when the early Christians began to write in Latin, they not only limited the sense of the word religion to this part of its original meaning, but so used it in this limited sense as to fit it in with their own theology, till it gradually becomes nearly a synonym first for Christianity, and then for Catholic Christianity. The completion of this revolution in meaning was, however, only opening the door to fresh modifications.

Thus we find St. Thomas Aquinas, in one place, defining religion as "goodness rendering to God the honour due to Him"; and in another as "the manifestation of that faith, hope, and charity toward God to which man is, above all, ordained." But as the monastic system grew, a "religious house" came to mean a monastery, a "religious"—that is a religious person—a member of a monkish order, a "going into religion" the taking of the vows, and even a "religion" an order of monks. Most curious is it to read the decree of the famous fourth Lateran council regretting the confusion brought about in the church of God by the diversity of "religions," and laying down that none should ferment a new "religion," but whoso desired to adopt "a religion," should select one of those already approved. Religion throughout this passage means simply an order of friars. An Irish Protestant, Archbishop Trench, finds in this use of the word a notable evidence of the moral contagion of papal domination, and asks "what an awful light does this one word, so used, throw on the entire state of mind and habit of thought in those ages!" Writers of all the numerous sects of Protestant belief have accordingly endeavoured to bring the meaning of the word religion back to those points which each of them regard as of vital importance.

But how can they hope to keep it there, and only there? For writers who discard the dogmas of Christianity endeavour to put a meaning into the word which will harmonise with *their* newer views of life. The author of *Ecce Homo* says that religion is "habitual and regulated admiration," or "worship of whatever in the known universe appears worthy of worship." Mr. Frederic Harrison defines it as "veneration for the power which exercises a dominant influence over our life." And Matthew Arnold found in it only "morality touched with emotion."

It is evident that man's definitions of religion will be precisely as numerous, as different, and as accurate as their own beliefs. There is only one definition which all must accept, the historical one, and the history of the word goes back a long way before Cicero, and is still, to-day, in the making. For the word is a convenient expression for a very complex set of mental conditions, including, firstly, beliefs as to internal and external mysteries (souls and gods)—secondly, the mental attitude induced by those beliefs—and thirdly, the actions and conduct dependent upon both. No one of these constituent elements of religion is stable. They are never exactly the same in any two individuals, even when these profess the same faith and live under the same conditions. The beliefs especially (which are independent, except in a very indirect way, of the will of the individual) vary, and that in a definitely progressive way, from century to century. And in those countries where the expression "religion" has once obtained currency, it has been always and must still, in the future, be applied to each new variation. The connotation of the word is determined by popular usage, and popular convenience.* It can never be limited by scholars or by the self-regarding definition of the apologists of any particular creed.

Of the paramount importance of religion, there can be no doubt. The life of every individual is profoundly affected by religious views and religious feelings, either his own or those of the people by whom he is surrounded, and there is nothing which so deeply affects the happiness of a nation as the predominant religion. It is not surprising, therefore, that the present revival of historical research should have been accompanied by a deep interest in the comparative study of the history of religious beliefs. And we may congratulate the Organising Committee of this scheme of lectures on their desire to bring before American students the latest results to which these enquiries have at pres-

* Professor Max Müller, in his *Lectures on the Science of Religion*, 1873, p. 287, talks of "the broad foundations on which all religions are built up,—the belief in a divine power, the acknowledgment of sin, the habit of prayer, the desire to offer sacrifice, and the hope of a future life." But popular usage has been too strong for him. No one of these five is found in Buddhism, yet he calls Buddhism a religion (p. 142 and elsewhere).

ent reached; and on the wisely thought-out arrangements which ensure to their efforts so great a measure of success.

To me, I confess, the choice your Committee have made of the first subject for exposition seems particularly happy. For it is precisely in India that, for us Westerns, the evolution of religious belief is most instructive. It can be traced there with so much completeness, and so much clearness; we can follow it there with so much independence of judgment, with so great an impartiality; and it runs, in spite of the many differences, on general lines so similar to the history of religion in the West, that the lessons to be learnt from it are of the highest value. Nowhere else do we find the records of a movement stretching uninterruptedly over more than three thousand years. Nowhere else has greater earnestness or so much ability been devoted so continuously to religious questions. Nowhere else has there been so much freedom of thought. Nowhere else has the evolution of religion been so little influenced from outside. Yet nowhere else do we find a system at once so similar to our own in the stages and manner of its growth, and so interestingly and absolutely antagonistic to our own in the ultimate conclusions it has reached. And nowhere else do we find so complete a picture of the tendencies and influences which have brought about the marvellous change from the crude hypotheses of the earliest faith to the sublime conceptions of such original thinkers as those who put the finishing touches to the beautiful Indian picture of the Palace of Truth.

Our own religious beliefs grew up in the basin of the Mediterranean. Jews and Greeks, assisted and influenced in no small degree by Egyptians, laid the foundations. All the most earnest culture of the West has only availed, through so many centuries, to build the superstructure. Ideas similar to the two main and essential conceptions which underlie the whole—the belief in "God" and the belief in the "soul"—are no doubt to be found throughout the world. But in three places only do we find these two ideas developed into systems which can bear comparison with our own, either in the manner or in the length of the period of their growth, or in the complexity and richness of the final result. These three places are Persia, China, and India.

Now, as to Persia, the original beliefs of the Akkadians are only now just beginning to be known. Even as modified and recast by the Assyrians, the records are still for the most part unpublished and untranslated, and the few foremost scholars of Zoroastrianism are not in agreement either as to the date of its sacred books or as to the part it played up to the final struggle when all was submerged under the flood of a ruthless Muhammadanism. The labours of many generations of scholars will be required to unravel this strange story, and to tell, with any fulness and accuracy of detail, the tragic tale. So in China history is almost a blank, a kind of battle-field for conjecture, before the time of Konfucius. Much has been done, no doubt, towards the elucidation of the religion founded by him on the more ancient faith. But Konfucius did not stand alone in China. We have only one work, of sufficient insight and authority, on the conceptions of Lao Tsü, which seem to the comparative student so much more original. And of the curious history of Buddhism in that country, of the influence it exercised on other beliefs, of the modifications it had itself to submit to, we have no systematic account at all. It is only in India that we have a very complete and authentic record, from a period more than fifteen centuries before the birth of Christ down to the present time, of the evolution of religious belief among a people practically isolated from the rest of the world. There remains, it is true, here also a great deal of important work to be done. But on the main lines at least the history is already remarkably clear. It is full of interest from the comparative point of view. And it reaches its culminating point in the Buddhist movement,—the main subject of the present course of lectures,—a movement which carried the evolution of religious belief one step farther than has been reached by any other of the numerous religions that history offers to our view.

That step—and it is a step of the first importance—is that Buddhism, alike in its ethics and in its views of the past and of the future, ignores the two theories of God and the soul. This came about in a very curious and instructive way. The oldest records in India (as is true also of the oldest records in every country that has records at all) show us a stage in culture in which the existence of gods and souls is taken for granted. The origin of these two theories is at present shrouded in mystery. Primitive man has left no records. We have only the evidence of those beliefs which are the later outcome of his crude hypotheses. And in attempting to read between the lines of these later records—even in the light, itself very meagre and uncertain, of the existing beliefs of very savage peoples—scholars are not altogether at one.

One or two principal points seem, amid difference of opinion as to details, to be generally admitted. Primitive man, whatever the race he belonged to, made no distinction at all between his experiences in everyday life and his experiences in dreams. And that was so, not because he looked upon life as a dream, but that he looked upon dreams as realities. When, in his dream, he saw a person he knew, on his awakening, to be dead, he at once concluded, on the mere evidence of his dream, that the person in question was still alive. And when he further recollected, as he sometimes must have done, that the body of the living man had been destroyed—his very nightmare may have been the result of his having feasted on the body of his foe,—then it was quite clear to him that there was a something (a breath, a life, he knew not what) which existed within the body, and was like the body, and which left it when the breath or life departed, to carry on a separate existence of its own. He did not reason much about it, or stay to consider whether its life was eternal or not. But he was too much frightened of it to forget it. And the dread reality afforded him a perfectly simple and a perfectly clear explanation of many otherwise mysterious things.

When he awoke in the morning after hunting all night in his dreams, and learnt from his companions that his body had been there all the time, it was of course his "soul" that had been away. The theory grew and flourished exceedingly. In all ancient books and in most modern ones too, and in travellers' tales about uncivilised and civilised men, we find it cropping up at every turn. Exactly how it grew, the order in which the applications of the theory took shape, is one of the battle grounds of the students of what is so oddly called Anthropology. To discuss the opinions on this point would take us too far from our subject. Suffice to say that the souls outside a man developed into gods. Souls were believed to wander from body to body. Animals had souls, and all things that men feared, and all that moved. The awe-inspiring phenomena of nature were instinctively regarded as the result of spirit action; and rivers, plants, and stars, the earth and air and heavens, became full of ghosts.

One distinguished writer who has turned aside from the easy devious paths of philosophy to the straight and difficult one of history, thinks that all gods were, in origin, the ghosts of ancestors. So uniform an explanation is most improbable. A much more solid basis seems to support the argument that as the oldest recorded gods are goddesses, and as man makes God in his own image, the original deities must have arisen at a time when women were the leaders, as in other things, so also in theology. They were born of women, for it was woman who conceived them. And we must make room in our theory at least as much for the awe inspired by Mother Earth, and by the mysteries of the stars, as for the worship of ancestors. We have to explain how it was that the oldest divinities were almost, if not quite, exclusively feminine. We have to explain why the moon was worshipped before the sun, and certain stars before either, and the Mother Earth before them all.

It is precisely the succession of these curious beliefs that is the interesting point. It was only among the advancing peoples that the changes went very far at all. And these changes are full of information about tribal conflicts and social conditions. For the gods had no existence except in the brains of their worshippers. They were *ideas*, a rough kind of scientific hypotheses. The arrival of a new god meant the birth of a new idea; and a book on *The Birth Days of the Gods* would be not only an epitome of human hopes and fears, but a history of men's views on social questions too.

For the gods, like the men who made them, grew old and feeble and passed away, and their very ghosts were degraded in the minds of the descendants of their creators to the rank of devils. The change in the object of worship was not merely a change in name, with the same or a similar worship; it was accompanied also by a change of view as to the relations of sex, as to mode of life, as to questions of organisation and government, and as to the forms of possession of goods and land. The worshippers of the new god thought themselves reformers, and often were so. The worshippers of the old gods looked upon the supporters of their rivals as atheists (just as the polytheists on the shores of the Mediterranean called the Christians atheists). But they were not in any case atheists, nor were they the founders of a new era, that was to last and to cure all woes. They only registered a new stage in the progress of thought, which (in this matter as in others) has, in the historic sense, an evolution of its own, independent of the men in whose brain the thought takes shape, and following (in all times and countries) precisely similar lines.

Many such changes had taken place in Indian spirit beliefs before the time of the oldest records that have come down to us. These show a very advanced stage in the ancient soul-theory. And there are no older records of its development along this particular line. The Akkadian records, it is true, go much farther back, and they have many points of analogy which seem to supply the actual historical origin of several later Hindu beliefs. But this is only because those beliefs have been incorporated into orthodox Hinduism from the descendants of those Dravidian peoples, related to the Akkadians, who preceded the Aryans in India. Nothing has yet been found in the Akkadian books showing any historical connection with Vedic beliefs.

On the other hand, we have in the ancient books of the Greeks and Persians, records of beliefs historically connected with the Indian. But these records are later in time than the oldest records in India, and preserve a later phase of the common beliefs. When we find, for instance, in the Zoroastrian books, that the hypothetical beings called in the Vedas "gods" have there already become "devils," we know that we have a later phase of a common belief. For it is the new religion which looks upon the gods of its predecessor as devils, and it is unknown that, in the course of the development of the same system of faith, devils should ever become gods.

The oldest Indian books—that is, the Vedas and Brāhmaṇas—therefore, though they themselves show us an advanced stage in ancient soul theory, are still the most ancient records of the particular line of development which we have to follow. And in them we find the germs of all the subsequent steps in philosophy and in religion that were taken in the valley of the Ganges.

The collection of Vedic hymns, as we now have it, bears of course no date. It resembles in this respect all other collections of similar antiquity, without exception, known to us. The date of the earliest books of each religion can be ascertained only by historical criticism, and so in India also. We have to start with facts that are known. We can argue back from the well established date of the great Buddhist Emperor of India, the famous Asoka. For we find in the literature extant in his time a series of strata, so to speak, of literary and philosophic activity, each of them indisputable evidence of the previous existence of the one before it. The last of these strata, the Buddhist Pitakas and the Sanskrit books of the same period, belong to his time. Estimates have been made of the previous interval that must be allowed successively for each of the other strata, between the time of Asoka and the close of the Vedic period, when the hymns were put into their present shape. And scholars are practically unanimous in the opinion that the Vedas must have been existing as we now have them at least 1000–1200 B.C., to allow time for the subsequent developments. Scholars also agree that they contain a good deal of material even much older than that, and the hymns stand in this last respect again on the same footing as the Buddhist

Pitakas, or the Old Testament, or any other ancient canon.*

They reveal to us a most interesting and instructive picture of a number of clans, closely related to ourselves, engaged in forcing their way into a country already more or less occupied, and occasionally turning aside from their contests with the darker natives to fight among themselves.

Judging from the hymns, the invaders—Aryans as we now call them—were intensely religious; but of morality, except as to customs within the clans, they seem to have had very primitive conceptions. To them the killing of opponents was no murder, and the "conveying" of their neighbour's goods a matter of pride. They have left us no idea on the rights of man (or of woman either); and in foreign politics their guiding principle was conquest. Within the clan, too, life was simple for them. There were no poor, and none too rich. They were not troubled with either priests or landlords. And the desire of their hearts was for increase in children, and in cows. The picture afforded us in the hymns of their daily life, and of their habitual thoughts, has a peculiar charm. It was a childlike and clearly a

* Attempts have recently been made to carry the age of the Vedas still farther back, by arguments based on supposed astronomical allusions. But the basis for these arguments seems very unreliable.

happy race, full of activity, and but little troubled by contemplation or by doubt. Probably even their religion sat lightly upon them, but it would seem from the hymns that they had an unhesitating and childlike faith, which looked upon the great souls animating the nature round them as all-powerful in their worldly affairs.

As time went on it is evident that some of them had however commenced to speculate on the nature of the gods, and had dimly begun to think that there was a unity underlying the manifold forms of spirit life in which the people believed. This is plain from those speculative hymns incorporated into the last and latest book of the great collection called the Rig Veda.

But it is also clear that the ancient Aryans were far too manly and free to be troubled much about their own souls, either before or after the death of the body. There are only a very few short and isolated passages bearing on this side of their spirit theory. They still held with a simple faith to the ancient hypothesis of their savage ancestors as to the existence of a "soul" inside their bodies. And it never occurred to them to doubt for a moment that these souls continued to exist in a sort of misty way after death, or to discuss the question of the duration or cessation of that future life. In all this we see the bright side of the ancient nature worship, of religion based on the soul theory as held in its early simplicity by a free and advancing and prosperous people. The darker side, which played in all probability a greater part in the daily thoughts and average life of the ordinary man and woman of those days, was that medley of strange beliefs and fears, revealed in the Atharva Veda,—the reliance on omens, and spells, and magic rites, the vague terrors of a life surrounded by all sorts of malign influences, the poisonous fruit of the superstitions of demonology.

While all these ideas, good and bad, were fermenting together, the bolder spirits were ever pushing farther and farther on into the hot plains of India. The details of their gradual progress are indeed hidden in an obscurity which we can scarcely hope now ever to clear up. But the general results are already well ascertained. Before the rise of Buddhism the whole of the country as far East as Patna, had become more or less Aryanised, either by alliance or by conquest, and the Aryan gods (that is to say, the men who worshipped them) held sway from the Kabul hills down to the plains of Bengal.

The religion was, however, not altogether uniform. As the tribes pushed on, their language, partly by the ordinary and necessary growth or decay, partly by intercourse with other peoples, continually changed. The favour of the gods was to be won only by the spell, as it were, cast over them by the faithful repetition of the ancient words. The words themselves had now become but dimly understood. Schools of priests had been formed to guard the words from destruction, not by writing—which was unknown—but by constant rehearsing. To aid them in their task, elaborate commentaries were composed and handed down, also by memory. Rules of grammar and of exegesis were devised and formulated into schemes of exposition. The whole intellectual power of the nation became for a time concentrated on these subsidiary studies. Works of original power, with the free and child-like spirit which animated the older hymns, became unknown.

The training in these schools was of a curious kind. History in our sense, and science too, were of course entirely unrepresented. The chief weight was placed on memory, and the ingenuity of commentators was much exercised in reconciling the diverse statements of the ancient texts—which could not err—and in finding mystic reasons to explain all the various details of the sacrifice.

Now one of the most striking things about the ancient hymns is the way in which each poet, partly no doubt through his want of expertness in the use of language, his inability to give due expression to shades of meaning; but partly also through the real fervour of his religious feeling, directed at the time on the one object of his praise—is the way in which each poet so often refers to different gods (Indra, Agni, Prajāpati, Varuṇa, etc.), as being, each one of them, the greatest and the best. There was not really any clear sense of comparison, though the words now seem to imply it. It was simply that the one God, that is to say, the one idea, loomed largest at the time before the mental eye of the poet. And in the explanation of such passages the Brahman Commentators carefully avoid all appearance of rivalry. A truer and—what was probably of more importance from the theologian's point of view—a more edifying explanation lay close to their hands. Already in the Vedas certain of the great souls, the gods, are identified with certain others, and there is even reference to a divinity which, as it were, lay behind them all, and was the basis of their godhead.

Thus there is a reference in the often quoted passage, Rig Veda, iii., 55, 1, to that "great godhead of the gods which is one." And the Brahmans gradually elaborated out of such expressions a conception of a single being out of whom all gods, and all men, and all things had proceeded.

It may be noticed in passing that a precisely similar result was reached, though not exactly by the same process, and at a slightly different chronological stage, in both Greece and China. And though we have no evidence of a like logical process in Assyria, it would seem that Egyptian thinkers also had their speculations of a similar sort. There is nothing strange in this coincidence. It is the exception of Assyria that is really curious. And we need not think to explain the coincidence by any theory of borrowing by anyone of these peoples from the other. For the fact is, that, whenever there is sufficent intelligence and sufficient leisure in a country where the soul theory is held, there, by a logical process which is inevitable, men will come to believe in a number of gods; and then, later on, to perceive a unity behind the many, and to postulate a single divinity as the supposed source of the many gods whom they themselves have really fashioned.

The characteristics of the new divinity, of the one god—that is to say, the connotations of the new idea—will differ according to the different conceptions out of which it has arisen. And in this respect the speculations of the Brahmans in India are especially worthy of consideration. With them the first conception was reached, not as among the Jews, by gradual additions to, and modifications of the character of one divinity, but by a purely philosophical reasoning as to the necessary nature of the first cause. The predicates they applied to him—or, more accurately, to it—were almost exclusively negative. It is the unknowable cause of the knowable, itself however without cause. It is the light in which all that is perceived is seen, but there is no light by means of which it can be seen. It is invisible, incomprehensible, without descent or colour, without eyes, or ears, or hands, or feet, the everlasting, all pervading, ever-present, extremely subtle, unchangeable source and support of all that is.* All the rest, including the great gods whom the ignorant worship and rightly worship as the highest that they know, is delusion. And the real insight, the only abiding salvation, consists in getting to know the impermanence of all else, and the identity of one's own soul with this Great Soul in which all else lives and moves and has its being.

There is great beauty and poetry in the passages in which this very ancient Pantheism is set out in the literature older than the rise of Buddhism, and though the exact formulation of this system of thought—well known as Vedāntism—is due to later hands, it is evident that there was much earnest thinking and fearless philosophising in the time of

* Muṇḍ., Up., i., 1, 5.

the oldest Upanishads in which these ideas find their earliest and most poetical expression.

The Indian formulation of this monistic theory of the universe is indeed in all probability the most logical and most thorough-going of all similar attempts that have been preserved to us. The very striking analogies in Greek philosophy, more especially in Parmenides (though he was a century later), cannot even be properly worked out owing to the fragmentary condition in which alone the earlier Greek speculations have survived. And the corresponding Chinese conceptions, either of the Konfucian or Taoist schools, seem to be altogether wanting in clearness and precision.

This very able and beautiful monistic philosophy was the dominant factor in Indian thought, when Gotama the Buddha appeared. Many centuries afterwards it was elaborated and systematised, more especially by Śankara, into that Vedāntist philosophy now quite supreme in India. In those early days it had no doubt stronger rivals. When the Pañcarātra books have been made accessible to scholars it will be found, I think, that they contain a systematic philosophy—built of the same cards, perhaps, as the Vedānta (god and soul)—but independent of it, and at least equal to it in beauty if not in logical power. We hear also of Lokāyatas, or Materialists, who must have preceded Buddhism, as they are mentioned in the oldest Buddhist books. The Jaina faith, which arose at the same time as Buddhism, has also a voluminous literature. When that is published it cannot fail to throw much light upon the religious life of India at the time when the founders of the two new religions were rivals. But there was little original thought in Jainism. Its views are rather isolated propositions than a system of philosophy, and it would never have been a formidable rival to Vedāntism.*

It was quite otherwise with the Sānkhya system. Centuries afterwards, when Buddhism had become corrupted, it would seem that the Sānkhya was almost about to supplant the Vedānta; and as it has often been held by European scholars that Buddhism is more or less based on the Sānkhya, it will be necessary to consider the question of its priority. Logically it stands half-way between the Vedānta and Buddhism, and was therefore a possible stepping-stone to the Buddhist position. And the Buddhists themselves acknowledge that Kapila, to whom the Sānkhya books ascribe the foundation of their philosophy, lived several generations before the Buddha. It is therefore, to say the least, pos-

* See the remarks of Professor Jacobi (and there could be no better authority) in his *Kalpa Sutra*, p. 3.

sible that the Sānkhya system also preceded the Buddhist, or was the outcome of the same intellectual movement.

But what we know is, that in the centuries immediately before and after the birth of Christ (that is, some centuries after the rise of Buddhism) it was the Sānkhya rather than the Vedānta, which was the predominant school; and that its adherents claimed a still more remote origin for their speculations. Professor Garbe, of Tübingen, who is the best authority on the subject,—he has done for the Sānkhya the same sort of service as has been so well rendered to the Vedānta by Professor Deussen, of Kiel,—is of opinion that the Sānkhya teachers are right, and that their teaching does indeed go back before the rise of Buddhism. The point seems to me, I confess, to be most doubtful. All the Sānkhya books are much later in date. The very oldest of them—the Sānkhya Kārikā of Īśvara Krishṇa—cannot be fixed at an earlier period than a full thousand years after the time of Gotama the Buddha. And though it is quite certain that the system, as a system already well worked out, was older than that,—we find it referred to, and in great part adopted, along with Vedāntism, in books, certainly two or three centuries older; in Manu, for instance, and in the Bhagavad Gītā,—yet there is still a great gap to be bridged over. All the available evidence on the point is collected, with great care and completeness, by Professor Garbe, in his just published *Sānkhya Philosophie*, a book which will, I hope, soon be translated into English. And on weighing all the evidence it seems to me that the only conclusion to be rightly drawn is that, though there is no evidence that Kapila was the real author of the whole Sānkhya philosophy, there were, before the time of the Buddha, isolated thinkers, of whose words we have no trace, who elaborated views similar to those out of which the Sānkhya was eventually developed.

For what do we find? There is ample evidence even in the books of the orthodox body of Brahman teachers to show that when Buddhism arose there was not only much discussion of the ultimate problems of life, and a keen interest in the result, but also that there was a quite unusually open field for all sorts of speculations. In no other age and country do we find so universally diffused among all classes of the people so earnest a spirit of enquiry, so impartial and deep a respect for all who posed as teachers, however contradictory their doctrines might be.

It is true that the orthodox books are filled with the orthodox view. But this is only quite natural. How very little of precise and accurate information do we find even in Christian books of the early centuries concerning the views of opponents? Even the Buddhist writings do not tell us much. But we have a detailed list in the first Suttanta of the *Dīgha Nikāya* of sixty-two different theories of existence; and in the second Suttanta of the same collection, the views of six leading opponents are discussed at length. I shall return to these passages later on. It is sufficient for the present argument to point out that they confirm in every particular the picture we find in the Brāhmanas and in the old Upanishads, and that one at least of the sixty-two views thus condemned seems to be a forecast of the Sānkhya. The passage is as follows—it is the Buddha himself who is represented as speaking:

"And in the fourth place, brethren, on what grounds and for what reason do the recluses and Brahmans who are believers in the eternity of existence declare that both the soul and the world are eternal?

"In this case, brethren, some recluse or Brahman is addicted to logic and reasoning. He gives utterance to the following conclusion of his own reached by his argumentations, and based on his sophistry.* 'Eternal is the soul, eternal is the world. They give birth to nothing; but are themselves unshaken as a

* For instances of this sophistry see the commentary.

mountain peak, as a pillar firmly fixed. And though these living beings pass along, transmigrate, fall out of one state of existence and are born in another, yet they *are* for ever and ever.' " *

Now this last is precisely the point in the soul theory on which the latter Sānkhya teaching differs from the Vedānta. According to the latter it is only God who is everlasting, the world is a phantom as it were, a dream, a delusion, and has its only real existence in God. And the souls themselves have no independent existence. They are God itself. But the Sānkhya on the other hand holds that there is no God, that the primordial Prakṛiti (or stuff out of which the world is formed) is eternal, and that the souls have a separate existence of their own, and continue to exist for ever in infinite numbers.

It will be noticed on the other hand that in the Buddhist description of this particular heresy the technical expression employed in the Sānkhya books for the primordial stuff is not used. It is here " the world " which the heretics are said to consider eternal, and that is not the view entertained by the Sānkhya. And if we should hold that the vague

* The Pali text will be found at vol. 1, p. 16 of the *Digha Nikāya* edited by myself and Mr. J. Estlin Carpenter, for the Pali Text Society in 1890. Buddhaghosa's commentary on the passage has also been published by us in the *Sumangala Vilāsini*, vol. i., pp. 105–107. (Pali Text Society, 1886.)

expression "world" may be taken here in the special sense of the "original matter" of the Sānkhya books, then we only come to another contradiction. According to the Sānkhya it is precisely out of the "original matter" and the individual souls that the visible world and living beings are produced. The heretics described in our passage hold that the soul and the world are barren, give birth to nothing. I am at a loss therefore to understand how this passage can be considered as good evidence that the Sānkhya system existed as a whole, just as we find it in books many centuries later, at the time when the passage was composed,—much less at the time of its legendary author, Kapila.

It is unfortunately impossible here to go into the details either of the Sānkhya explanation of *how* the world and living beings arose out of the original Prakṛiti (or matter) and the individual souls, or into the details of its psychological analysis. They also present very instructive analogies with the dualistic theories in Greece—analogies which will be considered of greater importance as the Indian side of the picture becomes better known. It is sufficient to point out there is nothing at all in any of the details peculiar to the Sānkhya which has been borrowed by Gotama, or is even to be found at all in any of the oldest Buddhist writings.

We have no body of writings other than those mentioned, to throw light on the religious speculations of India before Buddhism. But as regards the soul and salvation we have the very interesting list of the heresies on those points condemned by the early Buddhists, from which an extract has already been read. With your permission I will read this list. It does not follow, of course, that each one of the opinions quoted in it represents the teaching of a separate and distinct school. But the whole of it is full of suggestion as to the kind of discussions which were going on when Buddhism arose.

The extract occurs in a work of more importance than any other on Buddhism—the collection of the dialogues, mostly of Gotama himself, brought together in the *Dīgha* and *Majjhima Nikāyas.* This work contains the views of the Buddha set out, as they appeared to his earliest disciples, in a series of 186 conversational discourses which will some day come to hold a place, in the history of human thought, akin to that held by the Dialogues of Plato. The first of these 186 Dialogues is called the Brahma Jāla, that is the Perfect Net—the net whose meshes are so fine that no folly of superstition, however subtle, can slip through. In it are set out sixty-two varieties of existing hypotheses; and after each of them has been rejected, the doctrine of Arahatship is put forward as the right solution.

These sixty-two heresies are as follows:

1–4 *Sassata-Vādā.* People who, either from meditation of three degrees, or fourthly through logic and reasoning,* have come to believe that both the external world as a whole, and individual souls are eternal.

5–8 *Ekacca-Sassatikā.* People who, in four ways hold that some souls are eternal, and some are not.

a. Those who hold that God is eternal, but not the individual souls.

b. Those who hold that all the gods are eternal, but not the individual souls.

c. Those who hold that certain illustrious gods are eternal, but not the individual souls.

d. Those who hold that, while the bodily forms are not eternal, there is a subtle something, called Heart or Mind, or Consciousness, which is.

9–12 *Antānantikā.* People who chop logic about finity and infinity.

a. Those who hold the world to be finite.

b. Those who hold it to be infinite.

c. Those who hold it to be both.

d. Those who hold it to be neither.

* This fourth case is the one quoted in full above, p. 27.

13–16 *Amara-Vikkhepikā.* People who equivocate about virtue and vice.

a. From fear lest, if they express a decided opinion, grief (at possible mistake) will hurt them.

b. From fear lest they may form attachments which will injure them.

c. From fear lest they may be unable to answer skilful disputants.

d. From dulness or stupidity.

17–18 *Adhicca-Samuppannikā.* People who think that the origin of things can be explained without a cause.

19–50 *Uddhama-Āghatanikā.* People who believe in the future existence of human souls.

a. Sixteen phases of the hypothesis of a conscious existence after death.

b. Eight phases of the hypothesis of an unconscious existence after death.

c. Eight phases of the hypothesis of an existence between consciousness and unconsciousness after death.

51–57 *Uccheda-Vādā.* People who teach the doctrine that there is a soul, but that it will cease to exist

a. On the death of the body here.

b. At the end of the next life.

c.-g. At the end of subsequent lives.

58–62 *Dittha-Dhamma-Nibbāna-Vādā.* People who hold that there is a soul, and that it can attain to perfect bliss in the present world, or wherever it happens to be

a. By a full, complete, and perfect enjoyment of the five senses.

b. By an enquiring mental abstraction (the first Jhāna).

c. By undisturbed mental bliss, untarnished by enquiry (the second Jhāna).

d. By mental calm, free alike from joy and pain and enquiry (the third Jhāna),

e. By that mental peace plus a sense of purity (the fourth Jhāna).

The list is a formidable one, and it only trenches on certain selected points out of those that we know were the subjects of philosophical discussion in the India of that day. It must not be forgotten that we are dealing with an extent of country vastly greater than the region which was the seat, at a somewhat later period, of the beginning of Western philosophy. It is not only the numerous schools of the Brahmins in Middle India that we have to consider. We also must take into consideration the schools in the countries to the west of them (which the Aryans had left before the caste system had been established, and the Brahmin ritual had been developed), and the schools in the countries to the east of them where the Aryans, and no doubt Brahmins with them, had indeed penetrated, (which had been, so to speak, Aryanised,) but where the full power and influence of the Brahmins had not become so overwhelmingly predominant. It is precisely in these two regions, separated one from the other by a thousand miles of fertile and civilised plains, that we should expect to find the most unfettered thought, the widest dissension from the orthodox Vedāntist view, the most original and daring speculation. And it is not without significance that it is precisely there that in after years the two great universities of India were established—the one Takka Silā, in the extreme north-west, and the other, Nālandā, in Rajgir, in the extreme south-east.

I do not think, therefore, that the list I have read to you is at all exaggerated. The records of the thinkers referred to have all been lost. But this should raise no difficulty in our minds. Books were not written in India in those days. Even the wonderful powers of memory which those highly cultured people possessed, did not reach to learning by heart and handing down elaborate expositions of doctrines held to be insufficient or erroneous. To the life-long industry and marvellous memory of the scholars of that time, we owe the preservation of the extensive, and historically invaluable, literatures of the Vedic schools, and of the Buddhist Order; and instead of being astonished that the greater part of the rest has perished, we ought to be supremely grateful that so much has been preserved. After all, the old scholars of India, who were compelled to make a choice, were right in the choice they made.

These two systems are the highest expression, from the theological and the anti-theological points of view, respectively, of Indian thought. There is no one man to whom the original exposition of Vedāntist philosophy can be ascribed, no one name pre-eminent in pre-Buddhistic Vedāntism. But Śankar Ācārya, centuries afterwards, systematised and formulated the Vedāntist creed, and it is to Gotama the Buddha, that we owe what we call the Buddhist religion. There can be no doubt that these two, Śankar Ācārya and Gotama the Buddha, are the greatest names in the intellectual life of India, and that in preserving for us the records of the two systems of belief with which those names are associated, the repeaters of the Indian books have done for the world the greatest service they could do.

We have then in India in the valley of the Ganges, at the time when the Buddhist theory of life was first propounded, a maze of interacting ideas which may be divided for clearness' sake, into the following heads. Firstly, the very wide and varied group of ideas about souls, whether in man or in the lesser powers of Nature and also in animals, and even in trees and plants. These may be summed up under the convenient modern term of *Animism*, and include all the conceptions preserved in the books of astrology, magic, and folk-lore, the ideas of a future life and of the transmigration of souls, the beliefs as to all sorts of minor demons, and fairies, and spirits, and ghosts, and gods.

Secondly, we have the later and more advanced ideas about the souls or spirits supposed to animate the greater forces and phenomena of Nature. These may be summed up under the convenient modern term of *Polytheism*, and include all the conceptions as to the great gods preserved in the Vedas, and elaborated and explained in the Brāhmaṇas.

Thirdly, we have the still later and still more advanced idea of a unity lying behind the whole of these phenomena both of the first and of the second class, the hypothesis of a *One First Cause* on which the whole universe in its varied forms depends, in which it lives and moves, in which it has its whole and only being. This may be summed up in the convenient modern term of *Pantheism*. It is preserved in the Upanishads, and was subsequently elaborated and systematised by Śankar Ācārya.

Then we have the still subsequent stage now preserved in the already quoted Sānkhya books, and then probably already existing in earlier and less systematised forms, of a view of life in which the First Cause is expressly rejected, but in which with that exception the whole soul-theory is still retained side by side with the tenet of the eternity of matter. This may be summed up under the convenient modern term of *Dualism*. And we have slight glimpses of very numerous other views (among others of philosophies allied to what we now understand in the West by Epicureanism and Materialism).

These modern Western terms, though most useful as suggestions, never, however, exactly fit the ancient Eastern modes of thought. And we must never forget that these really contradictory explanations of the problem of life, now so carefully differentiated and kept apart by modern scholars, were not then mutually exclusive. We have to deal with a state of society in which, not history, nor science, but precisely these ultimate questions engaged the ardent attention and passionate patience of a surprisingly large number of men, of whom only a very few had the logical clearness and moral fearlessness to take a deliberate and exclusive stand. Just as afterwards the Vedāntist could accept parts of the Sānkhya position really incompatible with the rest of his belief, and both of them could believe in the actual truth, if not in the supreme importance, of animistic delusions. You will follow this the more readily inasmuch as a similar state of mind is still the most prevalent one in the West—when, for instance, a man may be a scientist and at the same time a spiritualist; or may accept the Darwinian hypothesis and the results of historical research, and also the substantial accuracy of the Hebrew cosmogony.

Such were the intellectual surroundings in which Buddhism arose. What I have had the honour of laying before you is of course the merest sketch. You will listen some day, I trust, to a whole course of lectures on Animism; to another on the Vedānta; to another on the Sānkhya; and to yet another on the remaining points of Indian belief in the sixth century B.C., to which allusion has been made. In the very narrow limits of time to which I am confined, it has only been possible to dwell on the more salient points, and I must apologise for having attempted to crowd so much into a single hour. But I have considered it my duty to bring out into as clear a relief as possible the points most essential to a right understanding of what *we* call Buddhism, and what the founder of that religion called the Dhamma, that is the Law, or the Norm.

Now the central position of the Buddhist alternative to those previous views of life was this—that Gotama not only ignored the whole of the soul theory, but even held all discussion as to the ultimate soul problems with which the Vedānta and the other philosophies were chiefly concerned, as not only childish and useless, but as actually inimical to the only ideal worth striving after—the ideal of a perfect life, here and now, in this present world, in Arahatship.

And I am only following the most ancient and the best of the Buddhist authorities in placing this most important point in the front of my exposition. The very first sermon which Gotama preached to his first converts is the Anatta Lakkhaṇa Sutta, (the discourse on the absence of any sign of "soul" in any of all the constituent elements of individual life) preserved in the *Vinaya*,* and recapitulated in full in the *Samyutta Nikāya*; † and translated by Professor Oldenberg and myself in our *Vinaya Texts*.‡ The very first of the collection of the dialogues of Gotama, forming the principal book on the Dhamma in the Buddhist Scriptures, is the one already quoted in which the Buddha so completely, categorically, and systematically rejects all the possible current theories about "souls." And later books of the first import-

* *Mahā Vagga*, i., 6, 38–47. † *Samyutta*, xxii., 59.
‡ *Vinaya Texts*, vol. i., pp. 100, 101.

ance follow the same order. The *Kathā Vatthu*, a book of controversy composed in the third century B.C., against dissenters within the fold, is one of the latest included in the Buddhist Scriptures. But it also places this question of the "soul" at the head of all the points it discusses, and devotes to it an amount of space which makes it completely overshadow all the rest.* So also with regard to the earliest Buddhist book after the canon was closed, the very interesting and instructive series of conversations between the Greek king, Menanda (Milinda), of Baktria, and Nāgasena, the Buddhist teacher. It is precisely this question of the "soul" that the unknown author makes the subject of the very first discussion in which Nāgasena convinces the king that there is really no such thing as the "soul" in the ordinary sense. And he returns to the subject again and again. I have no time left in which to read you these clear and decisive passages of this most ancient Buddhist author outside the Scriptures known to us. You can find them in full in my translation of the Milinda just published at Oxford,† and in abstract in my little manual entitled *Buddhism*.‡

* See my article on "Buddhist Sects," in the *Journal of the Royal Asiatic Society*, 1892. I am glad to be able to add that this work, so important from the historical point of view, is now being edited for the Pali Text Society, by Mr. Arnold C. Taylor.

† *The Questions of King Milinda*, vol. i., pp. 40, 41, 85–87; vol. ii., pp. 21–25, 86–89.

‡ Rh. D., *Buddhism*, 16th ed., 1894, pp. 95–98.

We cannot be far wrong in attaching weight to a view considered in these ancient and authoritative Buddhist books to be of such transcendent importance. It is precisely the not having grasped this essential preliminary to a right understanding of Buddhism that has rendered so very large a portion of the voluminous Western writings on the subject of so little value. And the point is historically also of the very highest interest, for the Buddhist position is the inevitable logical outcome of all discussion of the soul theory; and the Buddhists of course hold that in the West also people must inevitably come to the same conclusion when they have leisure to turn from the at present all-engrossing questions of the accumulation and distribution of wealth.

You will, however, understand that this apparently at first sight purely negative position is not the Dharma proclaimed by the Buddha. It is merely his answer to the previous religious and philosophical systems. Without the "soul" they, one and all, fall at once to the ground. And the point is only made of so much importance in Buddhist writings, because the Buddhist teachers held, and rightly held, it impossible, before the rubbish had been cleared away from the site, to build the new Palace of Good Sense. They held it impossible, so long as men were harassed by doubts and fears about their "souls," to induce in them the emancipated state of mind essential to a calm pursuit of the higher life; they held it impossible to stir men up to the ardent and earnest and hopeful struggle after a perfect life here and now, in this world, so long as they were still hampered, and all their virtue tarnished, by a foolish craving (that could never be satisfied, and would be a disaster if it could be) for an eternal future life in Heaven.

It must remain an open question how far this position is really negative. It is a matter to a great extent of degree. The rival theories are occupied, to the virtual exclusion of other matters, predominantly with questions of soul. Buddhism says that any real advance in ethical theory, and also in the practical conduct of life, really begins only when the delusions about the soul have been fully, and freely, and finally renounced. The rival theories purport to explain the origin and end of all things. Buddhism declares that everything has a cause; and that it is not only a sufficient, it is the only true, method, to argue from one cause back to the next, and so on, without any hope or even desire to explain the ultimate cause of all things. The most famous Buddhist stanza found engraved on ten thousand votive gifts to Buddhist shrines in India, says, that,

> "Of all the things that proceed from a cause,
> The Buddha the cause hath told;
> And he tells too how each shall come to its end,
> Such alone is the word of the Sage." *

But the positive side of the Dharma must be reserved to a future lecture. The present one is only intended to show the surroundings among which this remarkably original and interesting view took shape, and its attitude towards the rival theories, not only of that day, but also of our own.

* *Vinaya Texts*, i., p. 146.

LECTURE II.

The Authorities on which our Knowledge of Buddhism is Based.

HOW keen must have been the intellectual pleasure of that small band of scholars in the West of Europe, who, at the end of the fifteenth century, were able to appreciate the meaning and the value of Greek MSS. The taking of Constantinople by the Turks (1453) was the last step in a great catastrophe which threatened no less than destruction to the MS. treasures preserved in the Greek Empire, and death or poverty to their cultured if effeminate owners. The owners were scattered to the West, and their MSS. changed hands and found new homes. Whoever has had the good fortune to study the entrancing story of that time, more especially as it is focussed in the life of Scaliger, will be able to realise the vivid state of expectancy with which the advent of each new MS. was hailed. The scholars had a very considerable knowledge of what had been written in Greece, and lost in the West; and devoured each new MS. to see whether it would fill up any of the gaps. Too many of those gaps are, alas, still unfilled; and hope has almost faded away now. But in those days almost anything could be hoped for, and the indescribable charm of reading something quite new, of editing a work never edited before, of translating a book never translated before, was within the reach of all. Well we can now live a life of equal expectancy and hope, rewarded quite as often with an equal intellectual prize.

The discoveries that have been made in the ancient libraries of Mesopotamia will no doubt have some day become of even greater importance to the historian of human ideas and institutions than the MSS. acquired by the scholars of the Renaissance. For when completely understood and interpreted they will reveal a whole series of phenomena, independent of the Greek, and reaching farther back into the mists of antiquity. So also the discoveries in Egypt, made piecemeal from year to year, have the charm of constant expectancy in a very high degree. And now we have as a third factor of the same kind in the intellectual life of modern Europe, the gradual unveiling of that unique and original literature, which is our subject-matter to-day.

Compared with the Egyptian and the Assyrian, it has the disadvantage of youth. For the Pali books are no older than the Greek ones rediscovered in the fifteenth century. But they have the corresponding advantage of containing a rounded and complete picture of a new and strange religious movement, the outcome of many generations of intelligent and earnest thought, and of the very curious social conditions by which it was surrounded and furthered.

The story of the discovery of Pali is not without its interest. When in the thirties that most gifted and original of Indian archæologists, James Prinsep—clarum et venerabile nomen—,was wearing himself out in his enthusiastic efforts to decipher the coins and inscriptions of India, whilst the very alphabets and dialects were as yet uncertain, he received constant help from George Turnour, of the Ceylon Civil Service. For in Ceylon there was a history, indeed several books of history, whereas in Calcutta the native records were devoid of any reliable data to help in the identification of the new names Prinsep thought he could make out. It is not too much to say that without the help of the Ceylon books the striking indentification of the King Piyadassi of the inscriptions with the King Asoka of history would never have been made. Once made it rendered subsequent steps comparatively easy, and it gave to Prinsep and his co-adjutors just that encouragement, and that element of certainty, which were needed to keep their enthusiasm alive.

Turnour was of course much pleased. He was a very busy man, at the head of the Ceylon Civil Service. But he had most intelligent and learned native assistants at his command. And by their help he published in the Calcutta Asiatic Society's journal a short series of articles on the Pali books, and finally brought out in 1837 a complete edition of the text of the *Mahā Vansa* (or "Great Chronicle" of Ceylon) with a translation into English, and a most interesting introductory essay.

The value of this *editio princeps* was at once and widely acknowledged. But on the death of Turnour, no one was found to carry on his work. There was no dictionary of Pali, and no grammar worthy of the name. European scholars could not go out to Ceylon, and there enjoy the benefit of the help which had made Turnour's labours possible. His book remained, like a solitary landmark in an unexplored country, chiefly useful as a continual inducement to some scholar with ability and leisure to explore beyond. Only a few insignificant essays, nibbling inefficiently at the outskirts of the subject, appeared in Europe, till at last in 1855 Mr. Vincent

Fausböll came forward with an *editio princeps* of another Pali text.

Mr. Fausböll, now Professor of Sanskrit at Copenhagen, was then engaged at the University Library there, and it was a very bold undertaking to attempt such a task with the limited aids at his disposal. He chose, not an historical work, but a religious one, the *Dhammapada*, a collection of 423 verses mostly culled from the Buddhist Scriptures (a sort of hymn-book); and he published, with the text, not only a translation into Latin, but also very copious extracts from the ancient Pali commentary upon it. His work has been of the utmost service, and it is the second landmark in the story of our knowledge of Pali. It is pleasant to be able to remind the reader that the veteran scholar has steadily adhered to his first love. He subsequently brought out a number of specimens of that wonderful collection of ancient folk-lore included by a fortunate chance in the canon of the Buddhist Scriptures. And finding how great was the interest they excited, he has now, for many years, been printing an *editio princeps* of the whole collection. Five substantial volumes have already appeared, the sixth is well advanced in the press, and we may legitimately turn aside for a moment to send to Professor Fausböll our congratulations, and our thanks, and to express a hope, in the interests of historical study, that he will be spared not only to complete this *magnum opus*, but to add in other ways to the great services he has already rendered to historical research.

But to return to our story. After the publication of the *Dhammapada* by Professor Fausböll in 1855, the study of Pali again languished for a whole generation, and would in all probability have languished still had it not been for the third landmark in the history of our knowledge of Pali, the publication in two volumes in the years 1870 and 1873, of the Dictionary.

This great work was due to the self-sacrificing labour of Robert Cæsar Childers of the Ceylon Civil Service. Soon after his retirement in 1866 he set to work to arrange alphabetically all the words found in the *Abhidhāna Padīpikā*, a vocabulary of Pali in 1203 Pali verses, then already edited by Subhūti Unnānsē, a well known Ceylon scholar. In making this re-arrangement Childers carefully added references to, and also other words taken from, the published texts, and from scholarly European books on the subject of Buddhism. His work rapidly improved as it went on, and there can be no doubt that its completion was almost a necessary preliminary to any further serious work in Pali scholarship.

The points to which I would most especially desire to invite your attention in this slight sketch are, that up to the year 1870 only two Pali texts of any size or importance had appeared in editions accessible to scholars in the West; and that, of these two, only one was a book out of the Buddhist Scriptures, and that this one was a short collection of edifying stanzas, not composed as a book by themselves, but selected, without their original context, from other Buddhist books, then, in 1870, still buried in MS.

Nevertheless, the number of books, good, bad, and indifferent, published on the subject of Buddhism, was at that date very large. The reader will be able to judge how far they were likely to be of any permanent value when he calls to mind that no one of the authors of any one of these books had ever even read the Buddhist Bible in the original. Now I would not for a moment quarrel with the enthusiasm for the study of Buddhism which leads people to write so much about it. But surely an enthusiasm according to knowledge would lead people to devote their leisure, their ability, and their means, rather to the publication and translation of the sacred books themselves, than to discussions about their contents carried on in much the same way as some chess-players play chess, *sans voir*, without seeing the pieces. What we want then is the texts themselves, and not extracts or abstracts, but the whole texts. And we want also the whole of such aids to the right understanding of the text, as are still extant in the shape of ancient Pali commentaries, and even of more modern Pali treatises, written by Buddhist authors. To this aim—the publication and elucidation of the Buddhist texts —I have devoted what remains of my life; and I must trust myself entirely to your courtesy when I find myself here to-day—in spite of what I have just said, and have so often said before—turning away from that work to tell you how far it has got, what prospects it has of going on, and chiefly in some detail what is the nature and magnitude of the work that has to be accomplished.

A rough list of the Piṭakas, with notes on the contents of each book, will be found in my little manual of *Buddhism*,* and another list in my *Milinda* gives the number of pages, printed and not yet printed, in each of the twenty-nine books.† A similar list brought up to date is appended to this lecture.

From this last list it appears that the whole of the Piṭakas will occupy about 10,000 pages 8vo., of the size and type used by the Pali Text Society (about the same as these lectures). And from the calculations set out in the note to the list in *Buddhism* it

**Buddhism*, 16th edition. Appendix to chapter i.

†*Questions of King Milinda*, vol. i., p. xxxvi.

follows that the number of Pali words in the whole is about twice the number of words in our English Bible. These figures are sufficient to show the *extent* of the Buddhist Scriptures. To give an idea of their contents is not so easy, and it would be really impossible to frame any general description of the whole. The most accurate, and I believe also the most interesting method will be to run through the whole list (it is not a very long one), giving a paragraph or two to each. You will thus be able to realise what it is that the books do, and what is perhaps of more importance, what they do not, contain.

And firstly: The whole collection as we have it is divided into three parts, now called Piṭakas or Baskets. In that technical sense the word Piṭaka does not of course occur in the books themselves, just as the word Testament (in its technical sense of a division of the Bible) does not occur in the Bible itself. The meaning of the term Piṭaka or Basket is not to be taken in the sense of a thing to put things away in, like a box or other receptacle, but in the sense of tradition. Excavations in early times, and not in the East only, used to be carried out by the aid of baskets handed on from workman to workman, posted in a long line from the point of removal to the point of deposit. So we are to understand a long line of teachers and pupils handing on, in these three sacred Piṭakas or Baskets, from ancient times down to to-day, the treasures of the Dhamma (of the Norm).

The first of the three—the *Vinaya*—contains all that relates to the Order of Mendicant Recluses, how it came about that the Order was founded; the rules which the Brethren and Sisters have to observe, and so on. The second—the *Suttas*—contains the truths of the religion itself presented from very varied points of view, and in very varied style; together with the discussion and elucidation of the psychological system on which those truths are based. The third—the *Abhidhamma*—contains a further supplementary and more detailed discussion of that psychological system, and of various points arising out of it.

So much for the leading division into Piṭakas or Baskets. We will now consider the details of each.

Vinaya—the Canon Law—(literally "guidance") is divided into three partitions, the Sutta Vibhanga, the Khandhakas, and the Parivāra.

The word Sutta (sūtra in Sanskrit) is a very ancient literary term in India. The literal meaning is "thread," and it is applied to a kind of book, the contents of which are, as it were, a thread, giving the gist or substance of more than is expressed in them in words. This sort of book was the latest development in Vedic literature just before and after the rise of Buddhism. The word was adopted by the Buddhists to mean a discourse, a chapter, a small portion of a sacred book in which for the most part some one point is raised, and more or less disposed of. But *the* Sutta *par excellence*, is that short statement of all the rules of the Order, which is also called the Pātimokkha, and is recited on every Uposatha day. On that day, the day of the full moon, the members of the Order resident in any one district are to meet together and hear this statement of the rules read.

The 227 rules are divided into eight sections, according to the gravity of the matter dealt with, and at the end of each section the reciter asks the assembly, whether it is blameless in respect thereof, and receives the assurance that it is. If any member has offended, he has then and there to confess, and receive absolution, or withdraw. The completion of the recitation is therefore evidence that all who have taken part in it are pure in respect of the specified offences. And this is the origin of that second name, the Pātimokkha, which means the Acquittal, or Deliverance, or Discharge. A complete translation, with notes, of this statement of the Rules of the Order will be found in *Vinaya Texts*, the joint work of Professor Oldenberg and myself, contributed to the Oxford series of *Sacred Books of the East*.

This is the Sutta, of which the first book in the Vinaya, the *Sutta Vibhanga*, is the exposition in full—for that is the meaning of Vibhanga. The book deals with each of the 227 rules in order and following throughout one set scheme or method. That is to say it tells us firstly how and when and why the particular rule in question came to be laid down. This historical introduction always closes with the words of the rule in full. Then follows a very ancient word-for-word commentary on the rule—a commentary so old that it was already about B.C. 400 (the probable approximate date of the Sutta Vibhanga) considered so sacred that it was included in the canon. And the Old Commentary is succeeded, where necessary, by further explanations and discussions of doubtful points. These are sometimes of very great historical value. The discussions, for instance (in the rules as to murder and theft), of what constitutes murder, and what constitutes theft, anticipate in a very remarkable degree the kind of fine-drawn distinctions found in modern law books. These passages when made accessible, in translation, to Western scholars, must be of the greatest interest to students of the history of law, as they are quite the oldest documents of that particular kind in the world.

The second book in the Vinaya Piṭaka is called simply the *Khandhakas* or Treatises. It deals one after another with all those matters relating to the Order which are not stated in so many words in the Rules of the Pātimokkha. There are twenty of these treatises, and the points discussed in them are of the following kind:

1. Admission into the Order.
2. The Uposatha Ceremony and the Pātimokkha.
3. On retreats, to be held during the rainy season
4. On a ceremony called Pavāraṇā held at the end of the retreat.
5. On food, dwellings, etc.
6. On medicaments.
7. On clothes.
8. On the regulation by arbitration of differences of opinion.
9. On suspension and rehabilitation.
10. On the special rules for Sisters of the Order.

It would carry us too far to attempt a description in detail of these treatises. But I may describe one of them, as a specimen, and will choose that on medicaments, as it has an especial interest of its own.

The general rule as to the food of members of the

Order is stated quite clearly in the Pātimokkha. There was a slight repast of fruit and cakes, with milk or water as the beverage, in the early morning, no doubt very early according to our ideas. Then between 11 and 12 was taken the principal meal of the day, usually consisting of curry and rice, and great importance was attached to the regulation that this meal was not to be prolonged beyond the time when the sun cast a shadow.* In the latitude of the valley of the Ganges that means midday. After sunturn no more solid substantial food was to be taken that day. But slight repasts in the afternoon, and at what we should call supper-time, were allowed and practised. Now it became a pretty point of casuistry to determine what was solid food and what was not, and a longish list of things held permissible might be compiled from the earlier portions of the Khandhakas. Among the rest there was a considerable number of things allowed as medicine in the case of sufferers from certain specified diseases. And so in the Khandhaka or Treatise on this matter we obtain quite incidentally a very fair insight into a good deal of the medical lore current at that early period, that is about 400 B.C., in the valley of the Ganges. It is a pity that the cur-

* Pācittiya, 37; Khuddaka Pāṭha, par. 2; Culla Vagga, xii., 2, 8; Rh. D., *Buddhism*, pp. 160, 164.

rent authorities on the history of law and medicine have entirely ignored the details obtainable from these ancient books of Buddhist Canon Law. The whole of these Khandhakas have been translated by myself and Professor Oldenberg in the *Vinaya Texts* already referred to.

There is only one other book included in the canon under the head of Vinaya. This is the book called the *Parivāra* (or Appendix). It is very short, and is little more than a kind of student's manual, containing lists to assist the memory, and various sets of puzzles which are not unlike some modern examination papers. It is of course later than the other books on which it is founded, and is a very interesting bit of evidence on early methods of education.

The next great division is the Sutta Piṭaka, or the Basket of Discourses, and here we come to the sources of our knowledge of the most ancient Buddhism. The whole Basket consists of four great Nikāyas (or collections), and of these the first two form what we should now call a single book. It is in two volumes, so to speak, called respectively *Dīgha* and *Majjhima*—that is to say, long and of medium length (or to translate more idiomatically, longer and shorter). It contains 186 dialogues of Gotama arranged according to their length. They are discussions on all the religious and philosophical points of the Buddhist view of life. The Buddha himself is the principal interlocutor, but several of his principal disciples play a distinguished part in the book. In depth of philosophic insight, in the method of Socratic questioning often adopted, in the earnest and elevated tone of the whole, in the evidence they afford of the most cultured thought of the day, these discourses constantly remind the reader of the Dialogues of Plato. It would be worse than foolish to attempt any description of their contents. Each of the 183 dialogues would demand at least a single lecture to make its meaning clear. They have a style of their own, always dignified and occasionally rising into eloquence. It is a style intended, however, not to be read, but to be learnt by heart. You will easily understand therefore that it is a style intensely abhorrent to the modern devourer of newspapers and reviews and the last new novel. Scholars however will revere this book as one of the most priceless of the treasures of antiquity still preserved to us. And it is quite inevitable that, as soon as it is properly translated and understood, this collection of the Dialogues of Gotama will come to be placed, in our schools of philosophy and history, on a level with the Dialogues of Plato.

Ninety-one out of the 186 have now been edited

in the original Pali for the Pali Text Society, and about a dozen have been translated into English, seven of them by myself in the volume entitled "Buddhist Suttas" in the *Sacred Books of the East.*

A disadvantage of the arrangement in dialogues, more especially as they follow one another according to length and not according to subject, is that it is not easy to find the statement of doctrine on any particular point which is interesting one at the moment. It was very likely just this consideration which led to the compilation of the other two collections included in this Pitaka. In the first, called the *Anguttara Nikāya*, all those points of Buddhist doctrine capable of expression in classes are set out in order. This practically includes most of the psychology and ethics of Buddhism. For it is a distinguishing mark of the Dialogues themselves to arrange the results arrived at in carefully systematised groups. You are familiar enough in the West with similar classifications, summed up in such expressions as the Seven Deadly Sins, the Ten Commandments, the Thirty-nine Articles, the Four Cardinal Virtues, the Seven Sacraments, and a host of others. These numbered lists (it is true) are going out of fashion. The aid which they afford to memory is no longer required in an age in which books of reference abound. It was precisely as a help to memory that they were found so useful in the early Buddhist times, when the books were all learnt by heart, and had never as yet been written. And in the Anguttara we find set out in order first of all the ones, then all the pairs, then all the trios, and so on up to the thirty-four constituent parts of the human organism, or the thirty-seven constituent elements of Arahatship. It is the longest book in the Buddhist Bible and will fill 1800 pages 8vo. About two-fifths of the Pali text has been published by the Pali Text Society, and none of it has yet been translated into English.

The next—and last—of these great collections contains again the whole of the Buddhist doctrine, but arranged this time in the order of subjects. It consists of fifty-five so-called *Saṃyuttas*, or Groups, and in each of these a number of short chapters (Suttas), either on the same subject or addressed to the same sort of people, are grouped together. The Samyutta is divided into five volumes, four of which have been already published by the Pali Text Society, the fifth and last being in preparation. None of it has been translated into English.

It would be useless to speculate whether these two re-arrangements of the Buddhist doctrine are entirely dependent upon the Dialogues for their matter, or *vice versa*, or whether they are drawn also from other sources. We know that large portions of them recur bodily in the Dialogues, and that those portions not yet traced in the Dialogues contain nothing inconsistent with them. And it will not be very long before the publication of the whole of the three books, Dialogues, Anguttara, and Samyuttas, will enable us to state with accuracy the relation between them. This concludes the second Basket.

The third and last of the Piṭakas or Baskets, is the *Abhidhamma Piṭaka*, containing seven books of which at present only three have been published by the Pali Text Society. Abhidhamma has hitherto been rendered Metaphysics. But this is an entirely misleading translation. You will have realised from the previous lecture that the whole Buddhist view of life is constructed without the time-honoured conception of a soul within the body. We know nothing, according to Buddhism, except that which is derived from experience, the apprehension of phenomena. In such a system there is no room for Metaphysics at all. The noumenon is not discussed. What the Buddhists themselves understand by Abhidhamma is clear from the explanation given of the word by the great Buddhist scholar and commentator, Buddhaghosa. The passage, discovered by Mr. Arnold C. Taylor, has been edited and translated by him in a recent issue of the *Journal of the Royal Asiatic*

*Society.** According to that greatest of Buddhist scholars, Abhidhamma means merely the expansion, enlarged treatment, exposition in detail, of the Dhamma. And the Dhamma, as you know, is the Religion, the Truth, the Norm. The three books already published entirely, and the complete abstract of a fourth printed by me two years ago,† entirely confirm this view.

One, the *Puggala Paññatti*, or "Identification of Individuals," is a small tract of less than eighty pages, in which men and women are considered and classified from the ethical point of view. Another, the *Dhātu Kathā*, is on the bases of character, and discusses the mental characteristics most likely to be found in conjunction in converted and earnest folk.

The third already printed is the *Dhamma Sangaṇi*, or "Enumeration of States," and it analyses the states of mind reached by religious people, Buddhists and others.‡ The fourth book above referred to is the *Kathā Vatthu*, or "Account of Opinions," and is the only book in the Buddhist Scriptures of which

* *J. R. A. S.*, 1894, p. 560.

† *J. R. A. S.*, 1892, pp. 1–37.

‡ The commentary on this book, the first work of the celebrated Buddhaghosa, is just being edited for the Pali Text Society by Professor Ed. Müller of Bern; and a complete translation into English by Mrs. Rhys Davids, with introduction and notes, is in preparation.

we know the author and date. It was written (or rather put together, for books were not then written) by Tissa, the son of Moggali, about the year 250 B.C., at the Court of Asoka, the famous Buddhist Emperor of India. At that late period in the history of early Buddhism, the church or community was much torn by dissension and heresies. Asoka took great pains to restore the purity of the original faith. And Tissa, in furtherance of that object, refuted in this most curious ancient book two hundred and fifty-two of the most dangerous and important heresies put forward by the leading opponents of the orthodox school. There is nothing metaphysical in it. But it is most interesting from the comparative point of view that the most far-reaching cause of the decay of the primitive faith is here shown to have been the growth of what we should call superstitious views about the person of the Buddha. You will recollect how, in the history of the Christian Church, a very similar state of things existed, how the early Church was rent by dissensions arising out of the differing views as to the person of Christ, and as to his relation to the First Person in the Trinity. But in the Christian Church it was the new views, not found in the New Testament, that prevailed. In the Buddhist community, the new views were held at bay, and only succeeded, after a long interval, and in distant lands, in obtaining wide recognition. We shall have to deal with this subject further in our last lecture, so it need not detain us longer here. Mr. Arnold C. Taylor has nearly completed his edition of the *Kathā Vatthu* for the Pali Text Society, and has undertaken to translate it also.

We have now gone through the principal books in the Three Piṭakas, but there is a miscellaneous collection, mostly of shorter works, which has come to be included in the Canon. I have left this to the last, because Buddhists themselves from the very earliest times have been divided in opinion about it; some of them considering this Nikāya as an appendix to the Sutta Piṭaka, some of them considering it as an appendix to the Abhidhamma Piṭaka. The reason of this difference of opinion was probably something of the following kind. The most important things for the members of the Buddhist Order to preserve most carefully in their memory were essentially the Rules of the Community or Association they had joined, and the tenets of the Faith they professed. These were contained in the Canon Law, and in the Dialogues of Gotama, and in the various other books already referred to in which the doctrine set out in the Dialogues was re-arranged, elucidated, and expounded. During the time when the Canon was still unsettled, there was great activity in learning, rehearsing, repeating, and discussing these sacred books. But there was also considerable activity in what we should now call a more literary direction. There was a great love of poetry in the communities among which Buddhism arose. The adherents of the new faith found pleasure in putting into appropriate verse the feelings of enthusiasm and of ecstasy which their faith inspired. When peculiarly happy in their literary finish, or peculiarly rich in religious feeling, such poems would not be lost. They would be handed on from mouth to mouth in the small companies of the Brethren or Sisters, and some of them, either the oldest or the most popular, would gradually come to inspire so much veneration, so much love, that when the Canon was finally fixed, they could scarcely be left out. The question where to put them was however difficult. They could not, except in a very few instances, be inserted either in the books on the Rules of the Order, nor in the collection of the Dialogues of the Master. They must be added therefore either to the other parts of the Sutta Piṭaka in which the doctrine is set out, or to the Abhidhamma where the psychological side of it is enlarged upon in detail. It was not a point of vital importance, and we need not be too much surprised that some put these books as an appendix in one place, and some in another.

It was not only poems that found their way into this appendix. It contains at least one very ancient commentary ascribed to a famous leader and teacher in the Order. There is also a book on the Lives of the Saints, and another of ancient folk-lore. But the same sort of reason that led to the inclusion of the poetry, covered also these other works. And the whole collection is so very interesting as evidence of the literary life in the valley of the Ganges in those early times, that I hope you will allow me to devote a short time to each of these curious books.

The first, the *Khuddaka Pāṭha*, or "Short Recitations," is a little tract of only a few pages, starting with the so-called Buddhist creed:

> "I take my refuge in the Buddha,
> I take my refuge in the Religion,
> I take my refuge in the Order."

Then follows a paragraph setting out the thirty-four constituents of the human body—bones, blood, nerves, and so on,—strangely incongruous with what follows. For that is simply a selection of a few of the most beautiful poems to be found in the Buddhist Scriptures. There is no apparent reason, except their exquisite versification, why these particular pieces should have been here brought together. I cannot help thinking that this tiny volume was simply a sort of first lesson book for young neophytes when they joined the Order. In any case that is one of the uses to which it is put at present.

The *Dhammapada*, already mentioned to you (as having been edited by Professor Fausböll in 1855), is another of such selections, but this time not of entire poems. Here are brought together from ten to twenty stanzas on each of twenty-six selected points of Buddhist self-training or ethics. In almost all cases these verses, gathered from various sources, are here strung together without any other internal connection than that they relate more or less to the same subject, and the collector has not thought it at all necessary to choose stanzas written in the same metre or in the same number of lines. We know that the early Christians were accustomed to sing hymns both in their homes and on the occasions of their meeting together. These hymns are now irretrievably lost. Had some one made a collection of about twenty isolated stanzas, chosen from those hymns, on each of about twenty subjects—such as Faith, Hope, Love, The Converted Man, Times of Trouble, Quiet Days, The Saviour, The Tree of Life, The Sweet Name, The Dove, The King, The Angels, The Land of Peace, The Joy Unspeakable, and so on—we should have a Christian Dhammapada; and very precious such a collection would be. The Buddhist Dhammapada has been frequently translated. Where the verses deal with those ideas that are common ground to Christians and Buddhists, the versions are easily intelligible and some of the verses appeal very strongly to the Western sense of religious beauty. Where the stanzas are full of the technical terms of the Buddhist system of self-culture and self-control, it is often impossible, without expansions that spoil the set of the thought, or learned notes that ruin the poetry, to convey the full sense of the original. In all these distinctively Buddhist verses the existing translations are inadequate, and sometimes quite erroneous. The ancient commentary on these 423 verses tells a story about each of them, setting forth how, and when, and by whom, and on what occasion each of these stanzas was originally pronounced. These stories are written in very easy Pali and many of them are full of human interest. The late Dr. Wenzel and myself were preparing in collaboration a complete *editio princeps* of these stories—the copy is finished and nearly ready for the press, and will be issued as soon as I can find the time and the money. Cannnot some one undertake a translation for us into English of these strange and interesting old-world stories about a collection of verses so widely popular among Buddhists, and now attracting so much attention in the West?

As a general rule such stories explanatory of ancient verses—and without which very often the verses themselves would be quite unintelligible—were handed down in India by way of traditional comment. In two cases the Buddhists have included the stories themselves as well as the verses in the miscellaneous appendix to their Canon. One instance is the *Udāna*, or "Ecstatic Utterances." The Buddha is represented on various occasions during his long career to have been so much moved by some event, or speech, or action, that he gave vent, as it were, to his pent up feelings in a short ecstatic utterance, couched for the most part in one or two lines of poetry. These outbursts, very terse and enigmatic, are charged with religious emotion, and turn often on some subtle point of Arahatship, that is of the Buddhist ideal of life. The original text has been published by the Pali Text Society. But the little book—a garland of fifty of these gems—has not yet been translated.

The other instance (also edited but not translated) is the *Iti Vuttakam*. This contains 120 short passages, each of them leading up to a terse, deep saying of the Buddha's, and introduced in each case with the words *Iti Vuttam Bhagavatā*, "Thus was it said by the Blessed One." It is always invidious to look a gift horse in the mouth, and even did we wish to do so, the time has not yet come to discuss with profit whether these sayings were actually said as here represented. What we know, is, that these (often delicately beautiful) puzzles of thought on some of the deepest questions of human life were actually extant and so widely known and appreciated that they were included in the Canon, when the Canon was finally fixed. I think it would be impossible to assign them to a later date than 400 B.C., and I have no hesitation in saying that, at that time, there had been produced nowhere in the world any works approaching to these four booklets in delicacy of construction, in exquisite beauty of terse enigmatic expression, in depth of earnestness, and in real grasp of the most difficult problems that mankind has had to face.

These ecstatic utterances and deep sayings are attributed to the Buddha himself. There is also included in the Canon a collection (called, the *Thera-therī-gāthā*, or "Songs of the Elders," men and women) of stanzas attributed to 107 of the leading Theras (*i. e.*, Brethren), and 73 of the leading Therīs (*i. e.*, Sisters), in the Order during the lifetime of Gotama himself. The stories explanatory of the verses, giving a short account of the life history of each of the authors and authoresses, are handed down in the commentary. The commentary on the men's verses has not yet been published; but that on the women's verses has just been edited by Professor Eduard Müller, of Bern, for the Pali Text Society. With the help of this commentary my wife wrote an account of these Buddhist lady scholars for the Oriental Congress, held in London in 1892. It is published in the *Proceedings* of the Congress,* and affords a very instructive picture of the life they led in the valley of the Ganges in the time of Gotama the Buddha. It was a bold step on the part of the leaders of the Buddhist reformation to allow so much freedom, and to concede so high a position to women. But it is quite clear that the step was a great success, and that many of these ladies were as distinguished for high intellectual attainments as they were for religious earnestness and insight. A good many of the verses ascribed to them are beautiful in form, and not a few give evidence of a very high degree of that mental self-culture which played so great a part in the Buddhist ideal of the perfect life. Women of acknowledged culture are represented as being the teachers of men, and as expounding, to less advanced Brethren or Sisters in the Order, the deeper and more subtle points in the Buddhist philosophy of life.

As I have not so far troubled you with quota-

*London, 1894, vol. i., pp. 344 to 361.

tions, I venture to give the substance of two of these legends. The first is about Somā. She was born, says the Commentator, Dhammapāla, as the daughter of the Court Chaplain of King Bimbisāra at Rājagaha. Then, after taking the vows, she, with insight and good works, became an Arahat (that is, attained to Nirvana, the Buddhist ideal of the perfect life). Dwelling thus in the happiness of freedom at Sāvatthi, she entered one day the Andha Grove to pass the heat of the day, and sat there at the foot of a tree. Then Māra, the Evil One, wishing to frighten her from her meditations, stood there in invisible form and uttered the words,

"The vantage ground the sages may attain, is hard to reach.
With her two-finger test, woman cannot achieve those distant heights."

The Commentator pauses here to explain that what the Evil One refers to, is that women, though from their seventh year upwards they are always cooking rice, yet they cannot tell whether it has been boiled or not. They have to take some out in a spoon and squeeze it between their two fingers; then they know.

Now when she heard this the Therī rebuked the Evil One, and said:

"How should our woman's nature hinder us,
Whose hearts are firmly set, whose feet mount up
Unfaltering to those cool heights of Truth,
In growing knowledge of the Arahat way?
On every hand the love of pleasure yields,
Borne down by knowledge and the sense of Law,
And the thick gloom of ignorance is rent
In twain. Know this, O Evil One! and know
Thyself, O death! found out and worsted!"

Then the Evil One, thus rebuked, vanished away; and the Therī, strong in the sense of base suggestions overcome, continued in meditation till the cool of the evening.

The other poem is Sukkā's. Born of a wealthy family in Rājagaha, she became an adherent of the Buddha's, already in the first year of his public appearance as a teacher, and afterwards studying under another famous lady teacher (the Dhamma-Dinnā, whose story Mrs. Bode has told us in the *J. R. A. S.* for 1893), she was converted, and became an Arahat. She then attained to such mastery in exegesis and extemporary exposition that, in her hermitage near Rājagaha, she gave lectures open to the public, and gained great influence for good among the residents in her native city. Such was her eloquence as she taught, walking to and fro in her shady terrace, all who came from the city to see her, that the Dryad in the tree at the end of the terrace was filled with impetuous enthusiasm at her wisdom, and quitting its cool shrine, went off to Rājagaha and called aloud:

"What would ye men of Rājagaha have?
What have ye done? that mute and idle here
Ye lie about, like men bemused with wine,
Nor upon Sukkā wait, while she reveals
The precious truths of the Ambrosial way.
The wise in heart, methinks, were fain to quaff
That life's Elixir (once gained, never lost,
That welleth ever up in her sweet words)
E 'en as the wayfarer* welcomes the rain."

And when the people heard, they forthwith with eagerness went forth to Sukkā, and would not make an end of listening to her.

And when the Therī had reached her appointed span of life, and was about to pass away, she bore witness to the victory she had gained, and to herself, as to another person, uttered these words:

"O child of light, Sukkā, † by Truth set free
From cravings dire; firm, self-possessed, serene,
Bear to the end thy last incarnate frame;
For thou hast conquered Māra and his hosts!"

There is one instance, and one only, of a commentary, detached from its subject-matter, having been

* *Addhagu*, possibly the sun.

† *Sukkā* means bright, radiant, lustrous.

allotted a place among the Sacred Books. There must be some special reason for this. But it would be premature to discuss the matter till we have the text before us, and I am very happy to say that a distinguished American scholar, Professor Lanman of Harvard College, has undertaken an edition of this unique text for the Pali Text Society. It is called the Niddesa; and it is a commentary ascribed to Sāriputta, one of the most distinguished of the personal disciples of the Buddha, on the first part of the Sutta Nipāta. This last book, also included in our appendix to the canon, has been edited * and translated † by Professor Fausböll of Copenhagen. It consists of poems arranged in five books, the first four of which contain fifty-four separate poems, each of them only a page or two in length. But the fifth book is one poem almost certainly forming an independent whole. It is very unlikely that the other poems are all the work of the same hand. In all probability we have here another collection,—this time not of verses, but of complete hymns,—popular among the early Buddhists, but due to separate minds.

I hope to read to you in a future lecture translations of two of these lyrics.

* Pali Text Society, London, 1885 and 1893.
† Oxford, 1886.

There are two other short poems included in our appendix, each of them the work of one unknown author, and probably later than the other books in the appendix. One of these is the *Buddha Vansa*, poetical memoranda on the legends of the Buddhas supposed to have preceded the historical Buddha, the founder of Buddhism. The other is the *Cariyā Piṭaka*—a fragment never completed—giving a few short verses (scarcely more than an aid to the memory) on thirty-four of the supposed previous births of the historical Buddha himself. Both of these short, and from a literary point of view uninteresting, texts have been published for the Pali Text Society.

There are two other short poems in which legends regarding the future life are put into verse. They are called respectively the *Peta-* and *Vimāna-Vatthu*, and have been edited for the Pali Text Society, but not yet translated. Some of the longer legends are interesting as poems, and the whole set of beliefs exemplified in these books is historically interesting as being in all probability the source of a good deal of mediæval Christian belief in Heaven and Hell. But the greater part of these books, composed according to a set pattern, is devoid of style; and the collection is altogether of an evidently later date than the bulk of the books included in this appendix.

We now come to the *Jātakas*. These are stories nominally of the 550 previous births of the Buddha, but really a collection of the most popular folk-lore tales of all kinds—fables, fairy tales, riddles, puzzles, old-world legends, clever and witty judgments, instances of current superstitions good-humouredly laughed at, tales of magic cups and vanishing caps and wishing trees, stories of old mythology, and so on. At some period not quite ascertained, but certainly before 300 B.C., it had become the custom to identify the principal hero of each of these popular tales with the Buddha himself in a previous birth. It would be ungenerous to lay stress on the fact that this identification is entirely without foundation. For it is solely due to the fortunate chance of the growth of this idea that we have thus preserved to us the most complete, the most authentic, and the most ancient collection of folk-lore in the world—a collection entirely unadulterated, as modern folk-lore stories so often are, by the inevitable process of passing through a Western mind. Each story contains a stanza or stanzas attributed to the Buddha himself, either in his present or in his previous births. And it is only the verses that are included in the canon. They are usually unintelligible by themselves; but the comment, which gives the whole story in prose, gives also a further explanation of them; and Professor Fausböll edits the whole, text and commentary, together. I had at one time contemplated a translation into English of this most interesting, but also most voluminous work. The first volume of this translation appeared in 1881, under the title of *Buddhist Birth Stories.* But I have long been obliged to give up the hope of carrying on this work, and am now delighted to be able to say that a complete translation is being brought out by a syndicate of English scholars, under the editorship of Professor Cowell of Cambridge, and that the first two volumes, by Mr. Robert Chalmers and Mr. W. H. D. Rouse, members of the Pali Text Society, have just been issued by the Cambridge University Press.

There are one or two other books included in this appendix to the Three Piṭakas, but as they are not yet published, it would be premature to discuss their contents. You will have sufficiently understood the nature of the authorities on which our knowledge of early Buddhism must principally rest. You will have noticed that the rules of the Order—the books of Canon Law, if I may be allowed so to describe them—and the books of the Abhidhamma, the expansion of the psychological doctrines laid down in the Dialogues, are of historical rather than of literary value. But in the Dialogues themselves, and in some of the more ancient poems, we have documents of the first literary importance. You will have observed also that the contents of the books are not mythological, nor theological, nor metaphysical, but above all ethical, and in the second place psychological. You will have observed also that there is very little of what is popularly supposed to be the essential characteristic of religion—nothing about God and the soul, and the nature of them both, and the relation between the two. But Buddhism is none the less a religion; and it is the religion which comes nearest of all the other religions in the world to Christianity, and the religion which has influenced more lives than any other religion, not excepting even Christianity. It would not be the place here to discuss the doctrines of Buddhism, or to attempt to give the reasons of its great successes, and of its equally great failures. I shall have time in the subsequent lectures to lay before you the essence at least of its positive philosophy of life. Here I would only invite your attention to the fact that a small band of scholars are endeavouring, without pecuniary reward of any kind, to make accessible to the West the earliest documents of one of the most important and most interesting intellectual movements the world has ever seen. And I do not hesitate to appeal to you for your cordial sympathy with their self-denying labours.

When I returned from Ceylon, I made up my mind that, if my life was spared, I would try to get the whole of this literature edited and translated. When I began to speak of the advisability of starting a Pali Text Society with this object, I was told that the project was doomed to failure. No one cared enough for Pali to contribute the necessary funds; and even if they did, there were no competent scholars, not already otherwise engaged, to carry out the work. Well! the King of Siam, one of the most cultured and enlightened of sovereigns, sent me enough money to bring out the first volume; and private friends of my own showed their interest in historical enquiry by subscribing enough to bring out a second; and I soon had a small list of supporters, mostly poor men and scholars, willing to subscribe a guinea a year. This was enough for me to venture on a beginning. It was no easy task to find MSS. and competent scholars willing to spend years of labour without fee or reward of any kind. But both difficulties have been surmounted. The work has now gone on for twelve years. We have published thirty-four volumes, amounting in the whole to 7200 pages. Out of the twenty-seven books in the Buddhist Piṭakas, thirteen are now published in full, five others in part, one more is in the press, and nearly all the remainder are in preparation.

About one half of the work has been done, and the interest of scholars throughout the world has been so thoroughly aroused, that it is now only a question of money whether the work shall go on, and how soon it shall be completed. There are already three or four public libraries in Europe which have a fair collection of Buddhist MSS.; and I have a good many in my private collection, and correspondents both in Burma and Ceylon, who are helping to procure others as they are wanted. The number of scholars able and willing to co-operate in the undertaking is slowly but steadily increasing. But the printers will not work for nothing, and the only difficulty is the want of money to pay the printer's bills. Will not America come forward to assist in the important work of disentombing this ancient literature, now buried in MSS.?

I shall be happy to receive the subscriptions or donations of any one intelligent enough to see the importance of the work, and generous enough to give.*

* For the address of the Pali Text Society see the appendix to this lecture.

APPENDIX TO LECTURE II.

LIST OF THE PIṬAKAS.

THE VINAYA PIṬAKA.

NAME.		PRINTED PAGES 8VO.	ESTIMATED PAGES UNPRINTED.
1. The Sutta Vibhaṅga		617	None.
2. The Khandhakas—			
a. Mahā Vagga	360		
b. Culla Vagga	308	—668	None.
3. The Parivāra		226	None.
		1511	

THE SUTTA PIṬAKA.

4. The Dīgha Nikāya	261	600*
5. The Majjhima Nikāya	254	250*
6. The Saṃyutta Nikāya	1125	500*
7. The Aṅguttara Nikāya	560	1150
	2200	2500

THE KHUDDAKA NIKĀYA.

8. The Kuddaka Pāṭha	10	None.
9. The Dhamma Padas	40	None.
10. The Udānas	80	None.
11. The Iti-vuttakas	125	None.
12. The Sutta Nipāta	210	None.
13. The Vimāna Vatthu	84	None.
14. The Peta Vatthu	68	None.
15. The Thera Gāthā	115	None.
16. The Therī Gāthā	52	None.
17. The Jātakas	170	35*
18. The Niddesa	—	300*
19. The Paṭisambhidā	—	400*
20. The Apadānas	—	400*
21. The Buddha Vansa	60	None.
22. The Cariyā Piṭaka	30	None.
	1044	1135

* In preparation.

NAME.	PRINTED PAGES 8VO.	ESTIMATED PAGES UNPRINTED
THE ABHIDHAMMA PIṬIKA.		
23. The Dhamma Saṅgaṇī	264	None.
24. The Vibhanga	—	300*
25. The Kathā Vatthu	—	400*
26. The Puggala Paññatti	75	None.
27. The Dhātu Kathā	122	None.
28. The Yamakas	—	400
29. The Paṭṭhāna	—	600
	461	1700
Totals	5216	5335

ISSUES OF THE PALI TEXT SOCIETY,

22 ALBEMARLE STREET, LONDON, W.

I. ARRANGEMENT BY YEARS.

1882.

1. Journal.
2. Buddhavansa and Cariyā Piṭaka.
3. Āyāranga.

1883.

1. Journal.
2. Thera-therī-gāthā.
3. Puggala.

1884.

1. Journal.
2. Saṃyutta, Vol. I.
3. Sutta Nipāta, Vol. I. †

1885.

1. Journal.
2. Aṅguttara, Parts I.–III.
3. Dhamma Saṃgaṇī.
4. Udāna.

1886.

1. Journal.
2. Sumangala, Vol. I.
3. Vimāna Vatthu.

1887.

1. Journal.
2. Majjhima, Vol. I.

* In preparation.

† This volume was an extra volume presented as a gift to the subscribers in 1884. There are no copies left.

1888.

1. Journal.
2. Saṃyutta, Vol. II.
3. Aṅguttara, Part IV.

1889.

1. Journal.
2. Dīgha, Vol. I.
3. Peta Vatthu.

1890.

1. Journal.
2. Saṃyutta, Vol. III.
3. Iti-vuttaka.

1891.

1. Journal (1891–3).
2. Bodhi Vaṃsa.

1892.

1. Dhātu Kathā.
2. Paramattha-dīpanī.

1893.

1. Saṃyutta, Vol. IV.
2. Sutta Nipāta, Vol. II.

1894.†

1. Attha Sālinī.
2. Journal.

1895.‡

1. Kathā Vatthu.
2. Journal.

Total fourteen years: 36 texts; 38 volumes; 8400 pages.

II. Texts Published in the above Volumes Arranged Alphabetically.

	NAME OF TEXT.	YEAR.	EDITOR.
1.	*Abhidhammattha Saṃgaha....	1884	Prof. Rhys Davids.
2.	*Anāgatta Vaṃsa	1886	Prop. Minayeff.
3.	Anguttara, I.–III	1885	Dr. Morris.
	IV	1888	" "
4.	Attha Sālinī..................	1894	Prof. E. Müller.
5.	Āyāranga Sutta	1882	Prof. Jacobi.
6.	Buddha Vaṃsa.................	1882	Dr. Morris.
7.	Bodhi Vaṃsa..................	1891	Mr. Strong.
8.	Cariyā Pitaka..................	1882	Dr. Morris.
9.	* Cha Kesa Dhātu Vaṃsa......	1885	Prof. Minayeff.
10.	* Dāṭhā Vaṃsa	1884	Prof. Rhys Davids.
11.	Dhamma Saṃgaṇī..............	1885	Prof. Ed. Müller.
12.	Dhātu Kathā	1893	Mr. Gooneratne.

† In the press. ‡ In preparation.

	NAME OF TEXT.	YEAR.	EDITOR.
13.	Dīgha Nikāya, Vol. I..........	1889	Prof. Rhys Davids and Mr. J. E. Carpenter.
14.	*Gandha Vaṃsa..............	1886	Prof. Minayeff.
15.	Iti Vuttaka..................	1890	Prof. Windisch.
16.	Kathā Vatthu..................	1895	Mr. A. C. Taylor.
17.	Kathā Vatthu Commentary.....	1889	Prof. Minayeff.
18.	Khudda Sikkhā...............	1883	Prof. Ed. Müller.
19.	Mūla Sikkhā.................	"	" "
20.	Majjhima Nikāya, Vol. I.......	1887	Mr. Trenckner.
21.	*Pajja Madhu................	1889	Mr. Gooneratne.
22.	*Pañca Gati Dīpanā...........	1884	M. Léon Feer.
23.	Parāmattha Dīpanī............	1893	Prof. Ed. Müller.
24.	Peta Vatthu..................	1889	Prof. Minayeff.
25.	Puggala Paññatti..............	1883	Dr. Morris.
26.	*Saddhammopāyana...........	1887	" "
27.	*Saddhamma Sangaha.........	1890	Saddhānanda.
28.	Saṃyutta Nikāya, Vol. I......	1884	M. Léon Feer.
	Vol. II......	1888	" "
	Vol. III......	1889	" "
	Vol. IV......	1893	" "
29.	Sandesa Kathā................	1885	Prof. Minayeff.
30.	Sīmā Vivāda..................	1889	" "
31.	Sumangala Vilāsinī, Vol. I.....	1886	Prof. Rhys Davids and Mr. J. E. Carpenter.
32.	Sutta Nipāta, Vol. I..........	1884	Prof. Fausböll.
	Vol. II..........	1893	" "
33.	*Tela-Kaṭāha Gāthā..........	1884	Mr. Gooneratne.
34.	Thera Gāthā..................	1883	Prof. Oldenberg.
35.	Therī Gāthā..................	1883	Prof. Pischel.
36.	Udāna.......................	1885	Dr. Steinthal.
37.	Vimāna Vatthu...............	1886	Mr. Gooneratne.

NOTE.—Those texts marked with an asterisk are printed in the Journal.

The subscription to the Pali Text Society (22 Albemarle Street, London, W.) is one guinea *per annum*, payable in advance.

The publications are sent post free to subscribers.

Public-spirited friends of historical research have given donations amounting to about £450. Further help of this kind is urgently needed.

LECTURE III.

The Life of the Buddha.

IT is a strange thing, and very characteristic of the real meaning of the true Buddhism, that there is no life of Gotama the Buddha in the Buddhist Scriptures. Indeed the only work, so far known to us, that can be called a biography in our Western sense is a quite modern book called the *Mālālankāra Watthu*, of unknown date, but almost certainly quite two thousand years later than the Buddha himself.* There is a much older sketch of the first part of the Buddha's life, down to his thirty-sixth year, in the Introduction to the collection of Buddhist Folk-Lore called the Jātaka Book, and written about the fifth century of our era.† Both of these prose works rest on the same tradition, and are written in Pali, one in Burma and the other in Ceylon. Then there is a Pali poem called the Jina Carita,

*It has been translated into English by Bishop Bigandet under the title *The Life or Legend of Gaudama* (3d ed., London, 1887).

†This also has been translated into English by myself in the *Buddhist Birth Stories*, London, 1881, pp. 36-210.

"The Conqueror's Career," written in Ceylon by Buddhadatta in the twelfth century of our era, and dealing at length with the traditional episodes down to the thirty-sixth year, and also with the events of the last few months of the Teacher's life.* There are also two well known Sanskrit poems, the Buddha Carita and the Lalita Vistara, both of which have been translated, the first into English by Professor Cowell† and the second into French by Professor Foucaux.‡ The former, of which a portion is lost, can be dated with considerable certainty at the end of the first century of our era, and the second (though its date is unknown) is probably even later still.

These poems are not historical biographies. Milton's *Paradise Regained* is of value not for what it tells us about the life of its hero, but for the literary ability with which it has recast a story derived entirely from older documents. The historical value of those documents must be determined by a criticism which will, of course, take no notice of the later poetical version. A corresponding argument ought to hold good with respect to these Pali and Sanskrit poems, and *a fortiori* with respect to the Chinese and Tibetan reproductions of the San-

* Edited in the native character both in Burma and in Ceylon, but not yet translated.

† *Sacred Books of the East*, Oxford, 1894.

‡ *Musée Guimet*, Paris, 1888.

skrit ones. They are literary not historical documents, and such historical value as they have is the very instructive way in which they show how far the older beliefs about the life of the Buddha had been, at the time when these books were composed, developed (or rather corrupted) by the inevitable hero-worship of the followers of his religion.

It is unfortunately precisely these later Sanskrit poetical accounts which have been the source of modern popular notions about the life of the Buddha, and the beautiful poem of Sir Edwin Arnold entitled the *Light of Asia*, no doubt well known to many of you, is an eloquent expression in English verse of the Buddhist beliefs at the stage when those later poems were composed. Clearly the only proper course to pursue is to go back, behind these later poetical documents, to the actual text of the Three Piṭakas themselves, to collect there whatever is said incidentally about the life, family, and personal surroundings of the Buddha, and to piece them together into a connected whole. This has not yet been done, and cannot of course be done in a satisfactory way until the whole of the text of the Sacred Canon shall have been published by the Pali Text Society or elsewhere.

But certain progress has been made. There are accounts more or less circumstantial, in the introductory parts of many of the Dialogues, of various episodes in Gotama's career. Occasionally in an argument in support of one or another ethical proposition, autobiographical reminiscences are placed in the mouth of the Buddha himself as the principal interlocutor in the dialogue. Some of the ancient poems also relate to similar episodes, and in the introductory stories to certain of the rules of the Order, specifying the occasion on which the rule in question was originally established by the Founder, other autobiographical incidents are incidentally alluded to.

It will be impossible for me, within the limits of time at my disposal, to do more than summarise the results which can be reached from a comparison of such passages as these.

As you are all aware, the actual date of the birth of the Buddha is still a matter of controversy, but may be fixed approximately at about B.C. 600. He was born in the city of Kapila-vastu, about one hundred miles north-east of the city of Benares. This was one of those portions of the valley of the Ganges which had been the last to be brought under the influence of the Brahmins. It was far to the east of the Holy Land of Brahmin tradition, and there can be but little doubt that, at the time of which we speak, the inhabitants of that district were in many respects more independent of the Brahmins than the countries farther west. We have no evidence that there was any large number of Brahmins settled in the country, which was inhabited by a high-caste tribe, forming the Sākya clan. Mr. Beal, the late translator of so many Chinese Buddhist books, was of opinion that this very word "Sākya" was sufficient evidence to show that the clan was of Skythian, and therefore of Mongolian, origin. This seems to me a very wide conclusion to draw from a chance similarity of name, and also a very rash conclusion when so many details confirm the native tradition that the clan, or at least its principal members, was of Aryan descent. Its government was certainly aristocratic. We find indeed, in the sixth century before Christ, in the valley of the Ganges, a stage of social evolution very similar to that reached in Greece at the time of Plato. With one or two exceptions, kingdoms had not yet arisen. The country was politically split up into small communities, governed under republican institutions, some aristocratic, and some more democratic in character. These were just beginning to lose their independence by being merged into kingdoms formed by some successful despot. The later legends represent the Buddha as having been the son of such a king. But this is distinctly contradicted by the earliest documents. The texts are most particularly, almost ludicrously, careful to speak of everyone with the exact degree of reverence or respect due to their worldly position. Now Gotama's father is not spoken of as a king until we come to later documents,* whereas his first cousin, Bhaddiya, is addressed by the title of *Rāja*. Even Rāja, however, is not necessarily the same as "king" in English. It means "ruler," and may well have no stronger signification than that of "archon" or "consul."

The probability therefore is that Gotama was born in a family belonging to the highest ruling caste of the small Aryan community centred at Kapila-vastu in Kosala. The later accounts would lead one to infer that the Sākya domain was a rich and extensive country. There is nothing in the older books to confirm this opinion. Indeed, from the references to the adjoining states, it would seem to have been a small territory; not much more than 150 square miles in extent.

His people were agriculturists and, no doubt, the economic position even of the principal families among them was of a very simple kind. All the marvellous details of the wealth and glory of the royal palace, in which he lived in Oriental luxury,

* For instance Mahā Padhāna Sutta, and Buddha Vaṃsa (both included in the Canon).

are due to the natural desire to magnify the splendour of the position he renounced, when, for the sake of others, he "came out" as a mendicant teacher. The name of his mother has not yet been found in the oldest texts, but it is given in the Buddhavansa as Māyā, and we are told that she died when he was seven days old, and that he was brought up by his aunt, Mahā Pajāpatī of the Gotamids. We also know that he was married (though the name of his wife is not given), that he had a son named Rāhula, and that this son afterwards became an insignificant member of the Order founded by his father. Of Gotama's childhood and early youth we know next to nothing from the earlier texts. But there are not wanting even there descriptions of the wonders which attended his birth, and of the marvellous precocity of the boy. "He was not born as ordinary men are; he had no earthly father; he descended of his own accord into his mother's womb from his throne in heaven; and he gave unmistakable signs, immediately after his birth, of his high character and of his future greatness. Earth and heaven at his birth united to pay him homage, the very trees bent of their own accord over his mother, and the angels and archangels were present with their help. His mother was the best and the purest of the daughters of men, and his father was of royal lineage, a king of wealth and power. It was a pious task to make his abnegation and his condescension greater by the comparison between the splendour of the position he was to abandon, and the poverty in which he afterwards lived. And in countries distant from Kapila-vastu the inconsistencies between such glowing accounts, and the very names they contain, passed unnoticed by credulous hearers."*

Such legends are indeed of the greatest possible historical value from the comparative point of view. Similar legends are related of all the founders of great religions, and even of the more famous kings and conquerors in the ancient world. In a certain stage of intellectual progress it is a necessity of the human mind that such legends should grow up. They are due, in every case, to similar causes, and most instructive is it to watch those causes at work. I have dealt with this most interesting subject at considerable length both in my manual *Buddhism* and in my *Hibbert Lectures.* I have there pointed out the sources of the Buddhist Legend, and have shown how the two ideas of the King of the Golden Age and of the Prophet-Sage have influenced Buddhists in precisely the same way as the two ideas of the Messiah and the Logos have influenced Chris-

* Rh. D., *Buddhism*, 1894, pp., 182, 183.

tians, and how strikingly similar are the results attained by each. I will therefore content myself with referring on this occasion to those expositions, and will only remind you of the extreme importance of noting, not only the source of each particular incident in the legend, but also the date, as nearly as possible, when each episode became actually incorporated into the ever-growing tale. How long does it take people, perfectly sincerely and honestly, to believe in the Divine fatherhood of their hero, in his immaculate conception, in the extraordinary and even supernatural instances of the precocity of the child, and so on through all the list?

In this respect it is desirable to call attention to the publication by Mr. Robert Chalmers in the last volume of the Journal of the Royal Asiatic Society of the important text entitled the *Acchariya Abbhuta Sutta*, or "The Discourse on Wonders and Marvels." This is one of the dialogues referred to in the last chapter, No. 123 in the shorter collection. In it is laid down as true of each Buddha (and therefore also of the historical Buddha) that the universe is illumined with brilliant light at the moment of his conception; that the womb is transparent so that his mother can see the babe before it is born; that the pregnancy lasts exactly 280 days; that the mother stands during parturition; that on the birth of the babe it is received first into the hands of heavenly beings, and that supernatural showers provide first hot and then cold water in which the child is bathed; that the future Buddha walks and speaks at once, and that the whole universe is again illumined with a brilliant light. There are other details, but this is enough to show—as the collection of dialogues is certainly one of the very oldest texts we have—how very short is the time (less than a century) required for such belief in the marvellous to spring up.

We know that in his twenty-ninth year Gotama abandoned his home, his young wife, and his infant son, and went forth into the world to become a homeless wanderer, and to spend his life, first in thinking out for himself the deepest problems of experience, and then in spreading abroad to others the good tidings of the salvation which he deemed himself to have discovered. It may seem strange to western people, even of the most earnest and cultured sort, that any man, aiming at such results, should have thought it necessary to take this step. But the conditions of life at that time in the valley of the Ganges were very different from those obtaining at present. To work in one's study for the regeneration of mankind was almost impossible. There were no written books through which to communicate with the outside world. On the other hand the necessities were much fewer and much simpler. In that gorgeous climate and in that half occupied country, to retire into the woods and devote one's self to the higher life was not only practicable, but was even not uncommon. We hear of many instances of a similar kind. In the law-books, by which the lives of the Brahmins were regulated, it is considered so much a matter of course that a man should retire from the world, that the life of the good Brahmin is divided into three stages, during the first of which he is to be a student—during the second of which he is to marry, rear a family, and perform all the religious rites and sacrifices, and the household duties of a good Brahmin—and during the third of which he is to leave his home and retire, with or without his wife, into the forest, and live, as a recluse, a life of meditation. We are not unfamiliar, even among Christians, with the idea of a Retreat, into which a man may retire and, getting rid of the world, devote himself to the education of his heart. And at that time in India the doctrine of the Retreat was a favourite one, not only among Brahmins, but among the numerous sects which professed, each in a different way, to propound a solution, independent of the Brahmin theories, of the problems of life. We have constant reference in the

Buddhist books to wandering ascetics of every race and caste and sect, men and women alike, who wandered from village to village, and were ready to hold discussions with all the world.

Thus we are told, in the just published Paramattha Dīpanī, of a lady who was in the habit of wandering from village to village, and setting up at the entrance to the village a broomstick with the announcement, that she was willing to discuss with anyone who should overturn the broomstick. At one village which she reached a follower of the Buddha accepted her challenge. On the following day a public discussion was held between the two in the presence of all the village. The Buddhist answered all her puzzles, but she could not answer his, and full of confusion at a defeat (which for so many years she had never suffered) she threw herself at the feet of her opponent, and acknowledged herself a disciple from that day forth of the Blessed One. Again, in the Raṭṭhapāla Suttanta, one of the dialogues of Gotama, translated by Mr. Lupton, of the Indian Civil Service, in the *Journal of the Royal Asiatic Society* for 1894, there is a full discussion of the motives which led at that time in India to the adoption of such a life. Raṭṭhapāla, I may add, who is the recluse of this dialogue, is represented as young and rich, and in every sense of the word happy, when he retired from the world. And he explains to the king why persons should adopt this course from other motives than those of disappointment, poverty, or old age.

Having "gone forth," as the technical expression runs, Gotama went first to Rājagaha, the capital city of the neighbouring kingdom of Magadha. His visit is described in one of the ancient poems I have referred to as being included in the canon, and I will quote it as a specimen of the kind of biographical material we find in these records. It is called the *Pabbajjā Sutta*, and is contained in the Sutta Nipāta. Of course all the beauty of the rhythm in the Pali text of the simple ballad is lost in my prose version.

1. I will praise the homeless life, such as the Far-Seeing One led, such as when he had thought the matter o'er he deliberately chose as the homeless life.

2. "Full of hindrances is this household life, the haunt of passion; free as the air is the homeless state." Thus he considered, and went forth.

3. And when he had gone forth he gave up wrong-doing, both in action and in words, and he made his mode of livelihood quite pure.

4. To the King's town the Buddha went, to Girib-

baja in Magadha; full of outward signs of worth, he collected alms for food.

5. Him saw Bimbisāra, standing on the upper terrace of his palace. On seeing him with such signs, he spake as follows:

6. "Be careful, Sirs, of this man, handsome is he, great and pure; guarded in conduct, he looks not more than a fathom's length before him.

7. "With downcast eye, and self-possessed is he. Such an one is of no low caste. Let the king's messengers run forth and ask: Where is the mendicant going?"

8. Thus sent, the messengers hurried after him. They asked: "Where is the Bhikkhu going? Where does he mean to stay?"

9. Wandering straight on from house to house, guarded as to the door (of his senses), well restrained, mindful and self-possessed, he quickly filled his bowl.

10. When he had finished his round for alms the Sage went forth from the city, and gained the mountain Paṇḍava. "There shall my dwelling be."

11. On seeing where he stopped, there the messengers stayed; and one messenger went back, and told this to the king:

12. "The mendicant, O King, is now seated on Paṇḍava hill, like to a mighty tiger, like a lion in a mountain cave."

13. On hearing the messenger's words the prince in a state chariot hurriedly went forth towards the Paṇḍava rock.

14. And where the carriage road ended there alighting from his car, on foot the prince went on till he came near; and then sat down.

15. On sitting down, the King, with courtesy, exchanged with him the greetings of a friend. Then he spake thus:

16. "Young art thou and delicate, a lad in his first youth; fine is thy colour, like a high-born noble's,

17. "The glory of the vanguard of the army, at the head of a band of heroes. I will give thee wealth. Do thou accept it, and tell us thy lineage, when asked."

18. "Hard by Himālaya's slopes, O King, there is a country strong in wealth, the dwellers therein are of the Kosalas,

19. "Descendants of the Sun by race, Sākyas they are by birth. 'T is from that stock I have gone forth, longing no more for sensual delights.

20. "Seeing the danger therein, looking on going forth as bliss, I shall go on in the struggle, for in that my mind delights."

Here ends the Pabbajjā Sutta.

Having thus rejected the royal offer the recluse

placed himself as a pupil under one of the recluses who had established themselves in the mountains near Rājagaha. We have an account in the *Ariya Pariyesana Sutta*, given by Gotama himself,* of the essence of the teaching of this sage, whose name was Ālāra Kālāma, and of the reasons which led Gotama to be dissatisfied with the result.

He then went to another of these recluses, to Uddaka, the son of Rāma, but was again dissatisfied with the teaching that he heard.

We have other accounts of these two sages, *à propos* of certain propositions which they put forward, in passages of the *Saṃyutta*, in which similar propositions are discussed. From these passages it appears that the teaching of these masters was of no simple kind. It was an elaborately thought-out solution of the problems discussed (as already pointed out in our first lecture) by such later schools as the Sānkhya and Vedānta. And it is certainly evident that Gotama, either during or before this period, must have gone through a very systematic and continued course of study in all the deepest philosophy of the time. All the oldest accounts agree in stating that after working as a pupil under Ālāra and Uddaka, Gotama devoted himself, during a period the length of which is not known, to a regular system of what we should now call penance.

* *Majjhima Nikāya*, vol. i., pp. 163–5.

It was a matter of common belief at that time, that by the practice of austere self-mortification a man could compel the gods to manifest themselves to him and reveal the truth; and also that the suppression of bodily feeling would in itself open out the way to a greater vigour of the mind, and to extraordinary insight. From one or other of these motives Gotama accustomed himself gradually to live on smaller and smaller quantities of food, and, by checking and repressing his breath, sought to plunge himself into that state of trance in which he might experience the illumination that he sought for.

In carrying out these self-mortifications he was watched by five ascetics, who wondered at his self-resolution and waited to see him made partaker of the long-expected enlightenment. We need not, therefore, be surprised to learn that his fame is said to have spread round about like the sound of a great gong hung in the canopy of the skies.*

But he found himself no nearer the goal; and one day, after he had suddenly staggered and fallen in a faint to the ground, he determined to give up this method also, and again gradually to return to the ordinary life of a recluse. Then, when he was apparently most in need of sympathy, when his sense of failure might have been assuaged by the tender trust and respect of faithful followers, his

* Rh. D., *Buddhism*, p. 35.

companions forsook him, and went away to Benares. To them it was an axiom that mental conquest lay through bodily suppression. In giving up his penance he had to give up their esteem; and, in what might have been his sore distress, they left him to bear, alone, the bitterness of doubt.

There then ensued that mental struggle which culminated on the day when, under the Bo Tree, Gotama the recluse attained to Buddhahood and to Nirvana, deemed himself to have discovered at last the right solution of the mysteries of life, and became henceforth Gotama the Buddha. The later legends have described this, the most important event in Gotama's career, in poetical language not found in the earliest texts.* Even the well-known scene of the temptation by Māra, the Evil One (which fills so many pages in the later records, and in Sir Edwin Arnold's beautiful poem), is in those accounts entirely wanting. And when it is first incidentally referred to† we find only the bare men-

* The *Ariya Pariyesana Sutta* in the *Majjhima Nikāya*, vol. i., p. 167; and *Mahā Vagga*, i., i, 1 to i., 4, 5.

† In the *Book of the Great Decease*, iii., 42–45. Translated in my *Buddhist Suttas*, p. 53. Compare also the *Padhāna Sutta* in the *Sutta Nipāta* (Fausböll's translation, pp. 69–72) where the suggestion is quite different. The origin of this whole legend of Māra, to which we have two of these early references, inconsistent with one another. is perhaps to be found in the simple words at the end of the *Ariya Pariyesana Sutta* (pp. 174, 175).

tion of a suggestion to the Blessed One that now having solved the mystery, his work is done, and that the time had arrived for him to pass away without attempting to proclaim to others the glad tidings of the Noble Way.

But he rejected the thought (veiled under this figure of a suggestion from without), and resolved to preach his gospel to the world. First he sought out and proclaimed it to the five recluses who had been till lately his companions. In the oldest account of this episode * it is stated that when they saw him coming, they concerted with each other, saying:

"Friends, there comes the Samaṇa Gotama, who lives in abundance, who has given up his exertions, and has turned back to a life of ease. Let us not salute him, nor rise from our seats when he approaches, nor take his bowl and his robe from his hands. But let us just put there a seat. If he likes, let him sit down."

But when the Blessed One gradually approached nigh unto those five recluses, the five could not keep their agreement. They went forth to meet the Blessed One. One took his bowl and his robe, another prepared a seat; a third brought water

* *Mahā Vagga*, i., vi., 10, a little more expanded than *Ariya Pariyesana Sutta*, *loc. cit.*

wherewith to wash his feet, and a footstool thereto and a towel. Then the Blessed One sat down on the seat they had prepared.

Now they addressed the Blessed One by his name, and with the appellation "Friend." But he said to them: "Do not address the Tathāgata by his name, or by the appellation 'Friend.' The Tathāgata has become an Arahat, the supreme Buddha. Give ear, O recluses. The ambrosia has been won by me. I will teach you. To you I preach the Dharma (the Law, the Norm). If you walk in the way that I will show, you will ere long, having yourselves known it and seen it face to face, live in the possession of that highest goal of the holy life, for the sake of which noble youths give up the world and go forth into the homeless state."

They then object that, having given up his austerities, how can he claim to have gained the insight he had been seeking. But he repeats to them his assurance of knowledge; and when they again object, he says: "Do you admit that I have never unburdened myself to you in this way before this day?"

"You have never spoken so, lord," is the reply. He then sets out to them his view of life in a discourse called the *Dhamma-cakka-ppavattana-sutta*, or the "Foundation of the Kingdom of Righteousness."

In my next lecture I shall give you the actual words which he is related to have used on this important occasion, which the later accounts have surrounded once again with poetical legends which are sometimes of surprising beauty, and are remarkable as anticipating some of the very expressions used in the Christian legend of the day of Pentecost.*

The five recluses were converted to the new doctrine, and Gotama stayed with them in the hermitage near Benares. There he preached his doctrines and made other conversions until, after three months, the number of his disciples amounted already to sixty persons. Then he sends out his disciples † to wander through the villages, and preach the glorious gospel to the world; and himself goes on to Uruvelā with a similar purpose in view.

From this time his career as a teacher may be fairly said to have commenced. Henceforth till his death his mode of life was very simple. Like other recluses of the time he was in the habit of spending three months of each year—the three months of the rainy season—in residence at some particular spot. The other nine months of the year he wandered from village to village, through the valley of the Ganges, preaching and teaching his new gospel. I have not time, and it would be tedious, to attempt

* See my manual, *Buddhism*, p. 46. † *Mahā Vagga*, i., ii., 1.

to follow him through all these wanderings. It is true that, in each dialogue and poem, we have the account of the place at which it was spoken, and of the occasion which gave rise to it. But it is difficult to trace any chronological sequence, as the principal thing in the minds of the narrators has always been, not the time at which any word was spoken, but the portion of truth which it revealed.

We know that he returned eventually to his home, and very affecting is the account of his interview with his father, his wife, and his only son. And there are a number of other episodes which are both interesting in themselves as stories, and as throwing light upon the character of the Buddha. I have given in my Manual a statement of the most important of these episodes for the first twenty years of his career as a teacher. But I can here only deal with the more general features.

Now there is a very interesting picture in Buddhaghosa's commentary on the first of the Dialogues of Gotama, of the manner in which Gotama was wont, under ordinary circumstances, to spend each day. As this has never been translated, it may interest you to hear it. It runs as follows:

"For the Blessed One used to rise up early (*i. e.* about 5 A.M.), and, out of consideration for his personal attendant, was wont to wash and dress himself, without calling for any assistance. Then, till it was time to go on his round for alms, he would retire to a solitary place and meditate. When that time arrived he would dress himself completely in the three robes (which every member of the Order wore in public), take his bowl in his hand and, sometimes alone, sometimes attended by his followers, would enter the neighbouring village or town for alms, sometimes in an ordinary way, sometimes wonders happening such as these. As he went towards the village soft breezes would waft before him cleansing the way, drops of rain would fall from the sky to lay the dust, and clouds would hover over him, spreading as it were a canopy protecting him from the sun. Other breezes would waft flowers from the sky to adorn the path; the rough places would be made plain and the crooked straight, so that before his feet the path would become smooth and the tender flowers would receive his footsteps. And betimes a halo of six hues would radiate from his form (as he stood at the threshold of the houses) illuminating with their glory, like trails of yellow gold or streamers of gay cloth, the gables and verandahs round about. The birds and beasts around would, each in his own place, give forth a sweet and gentle sound in welcome to him, and heavenly music was wafted through the air, and the jewellery men wore jingled sweetly of itself. At signs like these the sons of men could know—'To day it is the Blessed One has come for alms.' Then clad in their best and brightest, and bringing garlands and nosegays with them, they would come forth into the street and, offering their flowers to the Blessed One, would vie with one another, saying, 'To-day, Sir, take your meal with us; we will make provision for ten, and we for twenty, and we for a hundred of your followers.' So saying they would take his bowl, and, spreading mats for him and his attendant followers, would await the moment when the meal was over. Then would the Blessed One, when the meal was done, discourse to them, with due regard to their capacity for spiritual things, in such a way that some would take the layman's vow, and some would enter on the paths, and some would reach the highest fruit thereof. And when he had thus had mercy on the multitude, he would arise from his seat and depart to the place where he had lodged. And when he had come there he would sit in the open verandah, awaiting the time when the rest of his followers should also have finished their meal. And when his attendant announced they had done so, he would enter his private apartment. Thus was he occupied up to the mid-day meal.

"Then afterwards, standing at the door of his

chamber, he would give exhortation to the brethren such as this: 'Be earnest, my brethren, strenuous in effort. Hard is it to meet with a Buddha in the world. Hard is it to attain to the state of (that is to be born as) a human being. Hard is it to find a fit opportunity. Hard is it to abandon the world. Difficult to attain is the opportunity of hearing the word.'

"Then would some of them ask him to suggest a subject for meditation suitable to the spiritual capacity of each, and when he had done so they would retire each to the solitary place he was wont to frequent, and meditate on the subject set. Then would the Blessed One retire within the private chamber, perfumed with flowers, and calm and self-possessed would rest awhile during the heat of the day. Then when his body was rested he would arise from the couch and for a space consider the circumstances of the people near that he might do them good. And at the fall of the day the folk from the neighbouring villages or town would gather together at the place where he was lodging, bringing with them offerings of flowers. And to them, seated in the lecture hall, would he, in a manner suitable to the occasion, and suitable to their beliefs, discourse of the Truth. Then, seeing that the proper time had come he would dismiss the folk, who, saluting him, would go away. Thus was he occupied in the afternoon.

"Then at close of the day should he feel to need the refreshment of a bath he would bathe, the while some brother of the Order attendant on him would prepare the divan in the chamber, perfumed with flowers. And in the evening he would sit awhile alone, still in all his robes, till the brethren returned from their meditations began to assemble. Then some would ask him questions on things that puzzled them, some would speak of their meditations, some would ask for an exposition of the Truth. Thus would the first watch of the night pass, as the Blessed One satisfied the desire of each, and then they would take their leave. And part of the rest of the night would he spend in meditation, walking up and down outside his chamber; and part he would rest lying down, calm and self-possessed, within. And as the day began to dawn, rising from his couch he would seat himself, and calling up before his mind the folk in the world he would consider the aspirations which they, in previous births, had formed, and think over the means by which he could help them to attain thereto." *

It is true that this picture is charged with supernatural details such as we must expect to find in

* *Sumangala Vilāsiṇī*, pp. 45–48.

the wording of a tradition which had been handed down for about a thousand years, but the expressions used are not without a certain poetical beauty of their own; and in the incidents which are here said to have filled up the time of the teacher, we have a picture substantially confirmed, as to its main features, by the incidental references in the earlier books. I have no doubt that this was actually the way in which the Buddha used to spend the working days of his useful and peaceful career; and that the tone of the narrative, the life of intellectual activity, the peace and harmony and gentleness pervading the picture, may be actually regarded as true. Of course we have here the description of a day spent altogether at one place, and it should not be forgotten that the Buddha was constantly moving about, and that then the hours of the early morning as well as of the close of the day would have been occupied, not in meditation, but in actual walking from one place to another.

There is one book or chapter, included in the Dialogues, and the longest of them all, which approaches in character to a gospel, and gives a detailed description of all the events of the last three months of his career. This Sutta* I have translated in full in my volume entitled *Buddhist Sut-*

* *The Mahā Parinibbāna Sutta* from the *Dīgha Nikāya.*

tas, and have analysed in my Manual. It is plain from this document, as well as from other passages in the earlier books, that, in his wanderings during the nine months of good weather, the Buddha was accustomed, as a regular practice, to walk from fifteen to twenty miles a day ; and this may account, in great measure, for the vigorous health which he enjoyed, and for the ripe old age to which he attained. He retired from the world at twenty-nine; he spent six years in study and meditation prior to his appearance as a teacher, and for forty-five years after that he lived this life of constant travelling, teaching, thinking. He had time, therefore, during this long period, to think out very thoroughly the views of life which are set out in the Dialogues and which will form the subject of our next two lectures. And by his constant intercourse with all the most cultured and earnest thinkers of the day through a large extent of territory, stretching from Patna in the south-east to Sāvatthi in the north-west, about three hundred miles long by one hundred miles in breadth, he had frequent opportunities of comparing his views with those of such men.

Moreover, by mixing daily with all sorts and conditions of men, from kings and wealthy merchants down to the peasants in the villages, as well as with Brahmins and leaders of sects, he was able, in an extraordinary degree, to enter into the needs and aspirations, the hopes and fears, of our common humanity.

It is very interesting, as evidence of the wonderful toleration which prevailed at that time, through the valley of the Ganges, that a teacher, whose whole system was so diametrically opposed to the dominant creed, and logically so certain to undermine the influence of the Brahmins, the parsons of that day, should, nevertheless, have been allowed to carry on his propaganda so ceaselessly and so peacefully through a considerable period of time. It is even more than that. Wherever he went, it was precisely the Brahmins themselves who often took the most earnest interest in his speculations, though his rejection of the soul theory, and of all that it involved, was really incompatible with the whole theology of the Vedas, and therefore, with the supremacy of the Brahmins. Many of his chief disciples, many of the most distinguished members of his Order, were Brahmins.

He admitted equally, it is true, men from all the other castes, and there were certain individuals, among the dominant school, who foresaw that this course of action would, in the long run, be fatal to the maintenance of the distinguished social position and pecuniary advantages of the Brahmins.

But on the whole he was regarded by the Hindus of that time as a Hindu. We hear of no persecution during his life, and of no persecution of his followers till many centuries afterwards. And it is a striking result of the permanent effect which this spirit of toleration had, that we find the great Buddhist Emperor Asoka, in his famous edicts, inculcating reverence to the Brahmins and to the teachers of rival sects, as much as to the leaders of his own persuasion. Throughout the long history of Buddhism, which is the history of more than half the people in the world for more than two thousand years, the Buddhists have been uniformly tolerant; and have appealed, not to the sword, but to intellectual and moral suasion. We have not a single instance, throughout the whole period, of even one of those religious persecutions which loom so largely in the history of the Christian church. Peacefully the Reformation began; and in peace, so far as its own action is concerned, the Buddhist church has continued till to-day.

But this is only one proof out of many of the fact we should never forget, that Gotama was born and brought up and lived and died a Hindu. His teaching, far-reaching and original as it was, and really subversive of the religion of the day, was Indian throughout. Without the intellectual work of his predecessors his own work, however original, would have been impossible. He was no doubt the greatest of them all; and most probably the world will come to acknowledge him as, in many respects, the most intellectual of the religious teachers of mankind. But Buddhism is essentially an Indian system. The Buddha himself was, throughout his career, a characteristic Indian. And, whatever his position as compared with other teachers in the West, we need here only claim for him, that he was the greatest and wisest and best of the Hindus.

[*Note on page 104.*—Since the above was in type Professor Windisch, of Leipzig, has published his very able and interesting monograph—*Māra and Buddha*, in which all the documentary evidence as to the growth of the legends about the relation of the Buddha to Māra is critically set forth.]

LECTURE IV.

The Secret of Buddhism.

Part I.—The Signs, the Path, and the Fetters.

YOU have all heard of the wonderful remains of Buddhist art which are the wonder and admiration of all travellers in India. Amongst the most striking of these ancient relics of a faith now forgotten in India are the Buddhist caves, the most famous of which have been discovered in the Centre and the West. There are the wonderful caves of Elephanta on an island in what was once a lonely bay, and has now become the busy centre of English trade in the East—the harbour of Bombay. There, remote from all the thronged haunts of men, the Indians of old hollowed out of the solid rock a number of apartments, some of them small, some of them so large as to be spacious halls, in which the recluses of that age might dwell far from the madding crowd, living a life of meditation and of peace. There are the still more impressive caves of Ajanta in Central India, where in a woody and hilly region now called the district of Nagpur, equally remote from busy life, the Buddhists of that time hollowed out the perpendicular face of a granite bluff, carving the entrance like some cathedral doorway and façade, and the interior into a series of lecture-halls and dwelling-places, supported by pillars left untouched in the solid rock, and ornamented with elaborate carvings and paintings, which make these caves one of the wonders of the world. Abandoned for centuries, the frescoes have yielded to the ravages of time, until in many instances, it is difficult to recognise what the artists intended to depict. I am glad to say that the School of Art at Bombay has made careful copies of what remains of these precious records of the past, and it is a great pity that these copies have not been reproduced in lithograph so as to make them accessible to scholars throughout the world.

One of the pictures so copied was long supposed to be an ancient representation of the signs of the Zodiac, and it is so called in the Bombay copy. It gives the figure, unfortunately in a very incomplete state, of a wheel divided into six compartments separated by spokes, and containing figures both in these compartments and around the rim. Mr. Waddell, of the Indian Medical Service, has shown in an article read this year before the Royal Asiatic

Society of England, that the subject of this curious fresco is not anything so material as the signs of the Zodiac at all, but is an attempt to represent the so-called "Wheel of Life" or "Chain of Causation." Gotama in one of the most ancient of the Buddhist texts,* is said to have thought out this wheel in that supreme moment of his life when, sitting under the Bo Tree, he attained to that high degree of insight which gave him his name of "The Buddha," "The Enlightened One." There is no doubt about this result, Dr. Waddell having discovered in Thibet an almost exact reproduction of this ancient picture, which reproduction being both complete and intact is readily intelligible.

I will read you from the Mahā Vagga the words in which this "Wheel of Life" or "Chain of Causation" was first formulated, and I venture to predict that though it is written in English, you will not understand a word of it.

"From Ignorance spring the Sankhāras.

"From the Sankhāras springs Consciousness.

"From Consciousness spring Name and Form.

"From Name and Form spring the Six Provinces (of the six senses).

"From the Six Provinces springs Contact.

"From Contact springs Sensation.

* *Vinaya*, i., 1.

"From Sensation springs Thirst (or Desire).

"From Thirst springs Attachment.

"From Attachment springs Existence.

"From Existence springs Birth.

"From Birth spring Old Age and Death, grief, lamentation, suffering, dejection, and despair." *

Now what does all this mean?

It would be impossible to explain it without first setting forth certain fundamental principles of the Buddhist doctrine which are here taken for granted and not expressed.

In the first place, it is an essential doctrine, constantly insisted upon in the original Buddhist texts, and still held, so far as I have been able to ascertain, by all Buddhists, that there is nothing, either divine or human, either animal, vegetable, or material, which is *permanent.* There is no being,—there is only a becoming. And this is true of the mightiest god of gods, as much as of the tiniest material atom. The state of an individual, of a thing or person, distinct from its surroundings, bounded off from them, is unstable, temporary, sure to pass away. It may last, as for instance in the case of the gods, for hundreds of thousands of years; or, as in the case of some insects, for some hours only; or, as in the case of some

* *Mahā Vagga*, i., 1, translated in *Vinaya Texts*, vol. i., pp. 75–77.

material things (as we should say, some chemical compounds), for a few seconds only. But, in every case, as soon as there is a beginning, there begins also, that moment, to be an ending.

In the lowest class of being, we have form of one sort or another, and various material qualities; in the higher classes, we find also mental qualities. The union of these constitutes the individual. Every person, or thing, or god is, therefore, a putting together, a component individuality, a compound, a confection (to coin an equivalent for the Buddhist technical term).* As the relation of its component parts one to another is ever changing, so it is never the same for two consecutive moments; and no sooner has separateness, individuality begun, than dissolution, disintegration, also begins. There can be no individuality without a putting together. There can be no putting together, no Confection, without a becoming different. And there can be no becoming different without, sooner or later, a passing away.†

Such thoughts are really quite familiar to us. We acknowledge them as true of all inorganic substances, and of living organisms, including our own. Geology has taught how the mightiest mountain chains, the

* Sankhāro.

† See for the orthodox Buddhist terms the notes in my *Buddhist Suttas* (Oxford, 1881), pp. 240, 241.

"eternal hills," and the deepest ocean depths grow into being and pass gradually away, as surely, and, compared with eternity, as quickly, as the gorgeous butterfly. Astronomy has taught us how the broad earth itself had once no individuality, and how, as soon as it began to be, it entered also on a progress of becoming, of continual change, which will never end till it has ceased to be. But the peoples of the West have inherited a belief in spirits inside their bodies, and in other spirits, good and evil, outside themselves, and to these spirits they attribute an individuality without change, a being without becoming, a beginning without an end. The Buddhists, like them, inherited from the Animism (the spirit theories) of their remote ancestors the belief in the existence of these external spirits. But the belief (which is not necessarily false because it is derived from the Animism of the savage) has not constituted in their minds any exception to the great Law of Impermanence,* the most important of the conceptions which underlie the Buddhist religion.

Buddhism goes even further, and says that all those subtle and excellent qualities, emotions, sentiments, and desires which make up the noblest life of man (and are now often referred to as "soul") are really discouraged and hindered by this belief in the

* In *Pali*, Aniccaṃ, see p. 43.

permanence and eternity of a semi-material soul. No training in ethics will be of any real advantage to the man who still nourishes this worst of all superstitions.

Secondly, it is a belief common to all schools of the Buddhists that the origin of sorrow is precisely identical with the origin of individuality. Sorrow is in fact the result of the effort which an individual has to make to keep separate from the rest of existence. To the universal law of composition and dissolution men and gods form no exception. The unity of forces which constitutes essential Being must sooner or later be dissolved; and it is to the effort to delay that dissolution that all sorrow and all pain are due. Wherever an individual has become separate from the rest of existence, then immediately disease, decay, and death begin to act upon it. Wherever there is individuality there must be limitation; wherever there is limitation there must be ignorance; wherever there is ignorance there must be error; wherever there is error there must sorrow come. As soon as an individual begins to be, the outside world plays upon that individual through the open doors of its six senses, sensations are stirred up within it, giving rise to ideas of attachment or of repugnance, and hence to a desire to satisfy the feelings so excited. Sometimes, more often indeed than not, it is impossible for the being thus affected to satisfy these cravings; it cannot gain what it wants, it cannot avoid what it dislikes. This inability involves pain or sorrow. Birth (the springing of the being into temporary individuality) is fraught with pain. It brings in its wake the liability to disease and to decay. And no separate entity can escape from change, disintegration, and at last from death. All these result inseparably from the struggle necessary to maintain and to carry on its separateness, its individuality. This is indeed, as I have elsewhere pointed out, a larger generalisation than that which says "A man is born to trouble as the sparks fly upward." It is an attempt to give a scientific explanation of the great fact of the existence of evil, and certainly the most consistent, if not the most successful, of all the efforts that have been made in that direction.

The third doctrine only applies and carries on these teachings of Buddhism with regard to individuality. It will be seen that individuality is not denied. The quarrel of the Buddhist teacher is against those delusions with respect to individuality by which all persons still in the animistic stage of thought are necessarily deceived. People naturally think that they are quite separate both from the world on which they tread, and from the people and other beings who inhabit it. They naturally think that they are separate both from all things and beings who have existed in the past, and all things and beings who will have their existence in the future. They even think that their own self is so important that it cannot possibly ever cease to be, and they are constantly concerning themselves with the ways and means of making that little self of their own happy and comfortable for ever. The Buddhist theory is, that these ideas are for the most part delusions; that men are blinded by delusion as to their separateness from the external world, that they are blinded by delusion as to their separateness from other beings in the past and in the future. Men overlook the fact that they are really no more separate than a bubble in the foam of an ocean wave is separate from the sea, or than a cell in a living organism is separate from the organism of which it forms a part. It is ignorance that thus leads them to think "This is I," or "This is mine," just as a bubble or a cell might think itself an independent being.

A watchman in a lofty tower sees a charioteer driving his horse along the plain. The driver thinks he is moving rapidly, and the horse in the pride of life seems to scorn the earth from which it thinks itself so separate; but to the watchman above, horse and chariot and driver seem to crawl along the ground, and to be as much a part of the earth as the horse's mane, waving in the wind, is a part of the horse itself. As a child grows up, its mind reflects as in a mirror the image of the surrounding world, and practically though unconsciously it regards itself as the centre round which the whole universe turns. Gradually its circle widens somewhat. But the grown man never escapes from the delusions of self, and spends his life in a constant round of desires and cares, longing for objects which, when attained, produce not happiness, but fresh desires and cares. With the majority of men these cares are mean, petty, and contemptible ; but even those whose ambition urges them to higher aims are equally seeking after vanity, and only laying themselves open to greater sorrows and more bitter disappointments.

So also it is with regard to the past and to the future. Men, dazed by the soul theory, and wrapped up in the present, are full of delusions about that. But they fail also to see that they are the mere temporary and passing result of causes that have been at work during immeasurable ages in the past, and that will continue to act for ages yet to come. It has been the great service which Comtism has rendered to humanity, that it has taught people to try to realise the solidarity of the human race. The Buddhist doctrine of Karma is an attempt made five hundred years before the birth of Christ to formulate a similar but wider idea. Men are merely the present and temporary links in a long chain of cause and effect, a chain in which no link is independent of the rest, can get away from the rest, or can really, as men think they can, start off, and continue to be by itself without the rest. Each link is the result of all that have gone before, and is part and parcel of all that will follow. And just as truly as no man can ever escape from his present surroundings, so can he never really dissociate himself, though he always takes it for granted that he can, either from the past which has produced him, or from the future he is helping to make. There is a real identity between a man in his present life and in the future. But the identity is not in a conscious soul which shall fly out away from his body after he is dead. The real identity is that of cause and effect. A man thinks he began to be a few years—twenty, forty, sixty years—ago. There is some truth in that; but in a much larger, deeper, truer sense he has been (in the causes of which he is the result) for countless ages in the past; and those same causes (of which he is the temporary effect) will continue in other like temporary forms through countless ages yet to come. In that sense alone, according to Buddhism, each of us has after death a continuing life.

It is worse than no use, it is full of hindrance to a man to

> "Inflate himself with sweet delusive hope"

in the impossible. And not only is there no such thing as an individuality which is permanent;—even were a permanent individuality to be possible, it would not be desirable, for it is not desirable to be separate. The effort to keep oneself separate may succeed indeed for a time; but so long as it is successful it involves limitation, and therefore ignorance, and therefore pain. "No! it is not separateness you should hope and long for," says the Buddhist, "it is union—the sense of oneness with all that now is, that has ever been, that can ever be—the sense that shall enlarge the horizon of your being to the limits of the universe, to the boundaries of time and space, that shall lift you up into a new plane far beyond, outside, all mean and miserable care for self. Why stand shrinking there? Give up the fool's paradise of 'This is I,' and 'This is mine.' It is a real fact—the greatest of realities—that you are asked to grasp. Leap forward without fear! You shall find yourself in the ambrosial waters of Nirvana, and sport with the Arahats who have conquered birth and death!"

This theory of Karma is the doctrine which takes

the place in the Buddhist teaching of the very ancient theory of "souls," which the Christians have inherited from the savage beliefs of the earliest periods of history. It is, at the same time, the Buddhist explanation of the mystery of Fate, of the weight of the universe pressing against each individual, which the Christians would explain by the doctrine of predestination. As I have said elsewhere: "The fact underlying all these theories is acknowledged to be a very real one. The history of an individual does not begin with his birth, but has been endless ages in the making; and he cannot sever himself from his surroundings, no, not for an hour. The tiniest snowdrop droops its fairy head just so much and no more, because it is balanced by the universe. It is a snowdrop, not an oak, and just that kind of snowdrop, because it is the outcome of the Karma of an endless series of past existences, and because it did not begin to be when the flower opened, or when the mother plant first peeped above the ground, or first met the embraces of the sun, or when the bulb began to shoot above the soil, or at any time which you and I can fix." A great American writer says: "It was a poetic attempt to lift this mountain of Fate, to reconcile this despotism of race with liberty, which led the Hindoos to say, Fate is nothing but the deeds committed in a prior state of existence. I find the coincidence of the extremes of Eastern and Western speculation in the daring statement of the German philosopher, Schelling. 'There is in every man a certain feeling that he has been what he is from all eternity.' We may put a new and deeper meaning into the words of the poet:

> 'Our deeds follow us from afar;
> And what we have been makes us what we are.'"*

It follows from the above that the good Buddhist cannot seek for any salvation which he is himself to enjoy in any future world. The result of his good actions, the fruit of his Karma, as the Buddhists would call it, will survive when he is dead, and advance the happiness of some other being, or of some other beings, who will have no conscious identity with himself. But, so far as he can reach salvation, he must reach it in this present world, he must enjoy it in this present life. The Buddhist books are constantly insisting upon the foolishness of wasting time (when there is so much to do, both for one's self and for others) in any hankering after a supposed happiness of heaven. And salvation here is precisely the being delivered from delusions with regard to individuality, in which the ordinary

* *Hibbert Lectures*, p. 114.

unconverted man is still entangled. When the mind has become clear from these delusions, a new and wider, brighter world reveals itself to the mind of him who has "entered upon the Path." And the Buddhist books are full of descriptions of the means which must be adopted first to get rid of the delusions, and secondly to gain the full heights of the peaceful city of Nirvana, in which he who is free from these delusions lives and moves and has his being.

It was necessary to explain these three fundamental ideas, or what follows would not have been understood; for, though much in them is undeniably true, and quite familiar to Western thought, yet the union of the three implies a view of life quite contradictory to the animistic notions accepted in the West. For, if the very conditions of individuality prevent its being permanent, and render inevitable its subjection to sorrow, then most of the Western ideas on the subject would require modification. And though the Buddhists do believe, in a sense of their own, in a future life, in the hereafter, yet that sense is so different from the one in which Christians use the terms, that Christian theologians would rightly class the Buddhists among those who do not believe in it at all.

For two essential conditions of a future life, as

held in the West, and indeed wherever the "soul" theory is in vogue, are the continuation of memory and the consciousness of identity. The "soul," in flying away from the body, is supposed, by those hypotheses, to carry with it the memory of these things at least which it recollected when in the body (and even, in some writers, of things which it had then forgotten), and to retain quite distinctly the sense of personal identity. The "soul" then enters upon a new life, either of weal, or of woe; and though there has of late years been much discussion whether the life of woe is permanent or not, there is no question either as to the permanence or the happiness of the life of those who are supposed to have entered the state of bliss. All this would be denied by the Buddhists. There is no passage of a "soul" or of an "I" in any sense, from the one life to the other. Their whole view of the matter is independent of the time-honored soul theories, held in common by the followers of every other creed. The only link they acknowledge between the two beings (in the one existence and in the next) who belong to the same series of Karma, is the Karma itself. The new existence is never either absolutely permanent or absolutely free from sorrow. And it is not a future life of the same being, but a new life of (what we should call) another being. For there is neither memory nor conscious identity to make the two lives one.

It would be a pretty piece of casuistry to say the Buddhist believes in a future life in our sense. But they are none the less earnest in their belief in it in their own. In that, it has been a deep reality to them, all through the long history of their faith, and in whatever age or clime their religion has been adopted. This is at least suggestive, in showing that one may pour a very different meaning into the terms "future" and "life," and yet they may still retain their influence over the hearts of men.

We have had thus far an explanation of three fundamental doctrines which are to be understood as underlying all Buddhist statements. These are the three doctrines of Aniccam, Dukkham, and Anattam, that is to say, of

The Impermanence of every Individual,
The Sorrow inherent in Individuality,
The Non-reality of any abiding Principle,

of any Soul in the Christian sense. How then did Gotama, having accepted propositions so fundamentally opposed to all that we are accustomed to find in our own religion, propose to solve the problem of salvation, to untie the knot of existence, to find a way of escape.

The solution was summed up in that memorable

discourse to his first converts, the circumstances of which were described to you at some length in the last lecture. I told you then how, in the discourse entitled the "Foundation of the Kingdom of Righteousness" the Buddha had laid down the essence of his system. This sermon has a merit very great in sermons, that of exceeding brevity, and with your permission I will read it you, omitting repetitions, and adding a few notes of my own.

"There are two extremes, O recluses, which he who has gone forth ought not to follow: The habitual practice, on the one hand, of those things whose attraction depends upon the pleasures of sense, and especially of sensuality (a practice low and pagan, fit only for the worldly-minded, unworthy, of no abiding profit); and the habitual practice, on the other hand, of self-mortification (a practice painful, unworthy, and equally of no abiding profit).

"There is a Middle Way, O recluses, avoiding these two extremes, discovered by the Tathāgata—a path which opens the eyes and bestows understanding, which leads to peace of mind, to the higher wisdom, to full enlightenment, to Nirvana.

"And which is that Middle Way? Verily it is the Noble Eightfold Path. That is to say:

"Right Views (free from superstition or delusion)—

"Right Aspirations (high, and worthy of the intelligent, worthy man)—

"Right Speech (kindly, open, truthful)—

"Right Conduct (peaceful, honest, pure)—

"Right Livelihood (bringing hurt or danger to no living thing)—

"Right Effort (in self-training and in self-control)—

"Right Mindfulness (the active, watchful mind)—

"Right Rapture (in deep meditation on the realities of life).

"Now this, O recluses, is the noble truth concerning suffering.

"Birth is painful, and so is old age; disease is painful, and so is death. Union with the unpleasant is painful, painful is separation from the pleasant; and any craving that is unsatisfied, that too is painful. In brief, the five aggregates which spring from attachment (the conditions of individuality and its cause), they are painful.

"Now this, O recluses, is the noble truth concerning the origin of suffering. Verily it originates in that craving thirst which causes the renewal of becomings, is accompanied by sensual delight, and seeks satisfaction now here, now there—that is to say, the craving for the gratification of the passions, or the craving for a future life, or the craving for success in this present life (the lust of the flesh, the lust of life, or the pride of life).

"Now this, O recluses, is the noble truth concerning the destruction of suffering.

"Verily, it is the destruction, in which no craving remains over, of this very thirst; the laying aside of, the getting rid of, the being free from, the harbouring no longer of, this thirst.

"And this, O recluses, is the noble truth concerning the way which leads to the destruction of suffering.

"Verily, it is this Noble Eightfold Path; that is to say:

"Right Views (free from superstition and delusion)—

"Right Aspirations (high, and worthy of the intelligent, earnest man)—

"Right Speech (kindly, open, truthful)—

"Right Conduct (peaceful, honest, pure)—

"Right Livelihood (bringing hurt or danger to no living thing)—

"Right Effort (in self-training and in self-control)—

"Right Mindfulness (the active, watchful mind)—

"Right Rapture (in deep meditation on the realities of life)."

Then with regard to each of the Four Truths, the Teacher declared that it was not among the doctrines handed down; but that there arose within him the eye firstly to see it, then to know that he would understand it, and thirdly, to know that he had grasped it; there arose within him the knowledge (of its nature), the understanding (of its cause), the wisdom (to guide in the path of tranquillity), and the light (to dispel darkness from it). And he said:

"So long, O recluses, as my knowledge and insight were not quite clear regarding each of these four noble truths in this triple order, in this twelvefold manner—so long I knew that I had not attained to the full insight of that wisdom which is unsurpassed in the heavens or on earth, among the whole race of recluses and Brahmins, gods or men. But now I have attained it. This knowledge and insight have arisen within me. Immovable is the emancipation of my heart. This is my last existence. There will be no rebirth for me.

"Thus spake the Blessed One. The five ascetics, glad at heart, exalted the words of the Blessed One."

The passages in brackets have been added chiefly from the commentary, for the reasons stated in my *Buddhist Suttas*. There is no doubt, I think, that we have here not only the actual basis of the Buddha's teaching, but also the very words in which he was pleased to state it. The early disciples who have preserved this record are not likely to have been mistaken on the first point, and the essential words of the discourse, however shortened, are not likely to have been much altered. The views here set forth are so remarkable as the basis of a religion promulgated in the sixth century B. C., that to suppose the disciples to have invented them is to credit them with a power of intelligence and imagination no less than that of their revered master. But to the historian it would be much the same thing whether the Foundation of the Kingdom of Righteousness were really due to the master or his followers. The remarkable fact is, that we have here set forth a view of religion entirely independent of the soul theories, on which all the various philosophies and religions then current in India were based; entirely free from the idolatries and superstitions of the day. And if this Buddhist ideal of the perfect life is remarkable when compared with the thought of India at that time, it is equally instructive when looked at from the comparative point of view.

We are struck at once with the analogy between it and the ideals of the last pagan thinkers in Europe before the rise of Christianity, and of some of the most advanced thinkers of to-day. And the similarity is no mere chance. It is due to the influence of similar causes. When, after many centuries of thought, a pantheistic or monotheistic unity has been evolved out of the chaos of polytheism—which is itself only a modified form of animistic polydæmonism,—there is a natural tendency towards the formation of a school in which theological discussions have lost their interest; and men have sought for a new solution of the deeper questions of life in a new system in which man was to work out, here on earth, his own salvation. It is their place in the progress of thought that explains why there is so much in common between the greatest philosopher of India, the Konfucian School in China, the Stoics of Greece and Rome, and some of the newest schools in France, in Germany, and among ourselves.

But we must not push the analogy too far. Each of these schools, though dispensing with the theologies, has peculiarities of its own, the result of the circumstances of its birth. None of the others are quite so frankly and entirely independent as Buddhism of the two theories of God and the soul. None of them have combined the conditions of self-mastery in quite the method or order found in the Noble Path. None of them have laid quite the same stress on the necessity of a co-ordinated activity of moral earnestness, emotional culture, and intellectual strength.

There is a sentence, often repeated in the oldest Suttas, which runs as follows:

"Great is the fruit, great the advantage of the rapture of contemplation (Samādhi) when set round with upright conduct. Great is the fruit, great the advantage of intellect when set round with the rapture of contemplation. The mind set round with intelligence is set free from the great evils—that is to say, from sensuality, from future life, from delusion, and from ignorance." *

Now we have here set forth in this Eightfold Noble Path the positive side of Gautama's ideal. In discussing the path in other Dialogues or Suttas, there is constant reference to the Ten "Samyojanas" or Fetters, which those who have entered upon the Path have gradually to break. It would complete the picture if I give you a short sketch of these ten points, though of course to make them fully clear one ought to have a lecture for each.

* See, for instance, *Book of the Great Decease*, i., 12; and my note on that passage in *Buddhist Suttas*, p. 11; and compare the Bhagavad Gītā, xii., 19; West, *Pahlavi Texts*, iii., 37; Sumangala Vilāsinī, 291, 298; and Anguttara Nikāya, iii., 86.

The first is the "SAKKĀYA-DITTHI," or Delusion of Self. After what has been said, you will easily understand what is implied by this term. And it is most significant that this delusion of self should be the very first fetter that the good Buddhist has to break, should be placed at the very entrance, as it were, of the path to perfection. So long as a man harbours any of those delusions of self which are the heritage of the thoughtless, so long is it impossible for him even to enter upon the path. So long as a man does not realise the identity of himself with those incalculable causes in the past, which have produced his present temporary fleeting individuality, so long as he considers himself to be a permanent being, and is accustomed to use the expression "This is I" and "This is mine," without a full knowledge of the limitations which the actual facts of existence impose upon their meaning, so long is it impossible for him to make any progress along the line of Buddhist self-culture and self-control. Until he has become fully conscious of the sorrow that is inherent in individuality, it will be impossible for him to begin to walk along the path which is the destruction of sorrow, and the end whereof is peace.

The next Fetter that he has to break is the fetter of VICIKICCHĀ, or Doubt. This is already defined in the Dhamma sangani (§ 1004), one of the books of the Abhidhamma, as being divided into eight divisions. It is doubt in the Teacher, in the Dhamma, in the Order; in the System of Training, and in the past, future, and present action of Karma, and in the qualities which arise from Karma. Having realised the impermanence of self and the sorrow wrapped up in individuality, he must be harassed by no doubts as to the insight of the Blessed One, or as to the efficacy of the means set forth in the Dhamma by which a man (working himself for himself, and being a lamp and a guide to himself) can, without relying on any external assistance, realise his aspirations after the higher life. In this connection I would like to read you a few words from the *Mahā Parinibbāna Sutta* (or *Book of the Great Decease*), addressed by Gotama, just before his death, to his favourite disciple Ānanda.

"Now very soon afterwards the Blessed One began to recover. When he had quite got rid of the sickness he went out and sat down behind his chamber, on a seat spread out there. And the venerable Ānanda went to the place where the Blessed One was, and saluted him, and took a seat respectfully on one side, and addressed the Blessed One and said:

"I have beheld, Lord, how the Blessed One was in health, and have beheld how the Blessed One had to suffer, and though at the sight of the illness of the Blessed One my body became weak as a creeper, and the horizon became dim to me, and my faculties were no longer clear, yet notwithstanding I took some little comfort at the thought that the Blessed One would not pass away until at least he had left instructions as touching the Order."

"What then, Ānanda? Does the Order expect that of me? I have preached the Truth without making any distinction between exoteric and esoteric doctrine. For in respect of the truth, Ānanda, the Tathāgata has no such thing as the closed fist of a teacher who keeps some things back. Surely, Ānanda, should there be anyone who harbours the thought, 'It is I who should lead the brotherhood,' or 'The Order is dependent upon me,' it is he who should lay down instructions in any matter concerning the Order. Now the Tathāgata, Ānanda, thinks not that it is he who should lead the brotherhood, or that the Order is dependent upon him. Why then should he leave instructions in any matter concerning the Order? I too, O Ānanda, am now grown old and full of years, my journey is drawing to a close, I have reached my sum of days, I am turning eighty years of age. And just as a worn out cart, Ānanda, can only by careful tying up be made to move along, so, methink, the body of the Tathāgata can only by much patching up be still kept going. It is only, Ānanda, when the Tathāgata, ceasing to attend to any outward thing, or to experience any sensation, becomes plunged in the rapture of contemplation that is concerned with no material object—it is only then that the body of the Tathāgata is at ease.

"Therefore, O Ānanda, be ye lamps unto yourselves. Be ye a refuge to yourselves. Betake yourselves to no external refuge. Hold fast to the truth (the Dhamma) as your lamp. Hold fast as a refuge to the truth. Look not for refuge to any one except yourselves . . . and whosoever, Ānanda, either now or after I am dead, shall act thus, it is only they among my recluses who shall reach the very Topmost Height, (that is, the Nirvana of Arahatship)—and even they must be willing to learn." *

It is perfectly clear from this striking passage that doubt in the Buddha cannot mean doubt in his ability to save. No man can save another. No one can save a man, save only himself. But the Master has discovered and shewn the way by which a man can save himself. It is that which constitutes his Buddhahood, and the doubt referred to is doubt in that.

* *Book of the Great Decease*, ii., 31-35, translated in my *Buddhist Suttas*, pp. 35-39.

And there is a good reason for the place this link, the link of doubt, occupies in the chain. To enter on the path one has to get rid, not of individuality, but of the delusions that cluster round the idea. When a man has seen through the mist, and realised that there is no permanent ego within him to gain an eternal paradise beyond the grave, then the temptation lies near, having found the old theologies wanting, to give up everything in despair, and betake himself to the lower life of ease and pleasure. Then is felt the necessity of confidence in the insight of the Buddha who has pointed the way along which a man may work out his own salvation, confidence in the adequacy of the Dhamma he has proclaimed, confidence in the reliability of the Order who hand it on, confidence in the unchangeable reality of the law by which the past and the future are bound in one.

The third Fetter is the Fetter of SĪLABBATAPĀRĀMĀSA, or of the efficacy of good works and ceremonies. It is essential that the man, who enters on the system of ethical training which we now call Buddhism, should begin by clearing away the rubbish of false beliefs, of sham supports which really afford no aid. Years ago, in Ceylon, when my old teacher Yātrāmullē Unnānsē was explaining this term to me, he let drop the admission that in his eyes Christianity came under this category. But of course in the early days of Buddhism the protest was against the existing rites and ceremonies then practised by the Brahmins in India; and it also included a protest (precisely similar to one that has often been urged by Christian theologians of the reformed schools) against the notion, that mere morality in the ordinary sense, the mere performance, however exact, of outward duties, can alone suffice.

To have broken these three Fetters constitutes what the Buddhists call conversion, a state of mind similar in its results, and in much of its connotation, to conversion as understood by Christians. A converted man, free from the delusions of self, from doubt, and from dependence upon works and ceremonies, is called technically the *sotāpanno*—he who has entered upon the stream. And having once entered upon the stream he can never be turned back. For the doctrine of the Final Assurance of the saints is part of the Buddhist system.

The fourth Fetter that he has to break is the Fetter of KĀMA (not Karma), or sensuality, bodily passions. This protest is common to all the ethical systems of the world; and the centre of interest from the comparative point of view is the degree in which the suppression of the bodily passions is inculcated in any one of them. In the Buddhist system we find that asceticism is as strongly objected to on the one hand as lust is on the other. You will have noticed that point in the first sermon, and also in the description of the Buddha's daily life. The Buddha himself is always represented as having been well clothed, well fed. And there are elaborate regulations in the rules of the order for the constant use of the bath, with which most of the hermitages were provided. Lay Buddhists were mostly monogamists, but the practice of celibacy and abstinence from intoxicating drinks was enjoined upon the members of the Order, and was a necessary condition of Arahatship. The point evidently is, that the mind should not be occupied either with the satisfaction or with the suppression of the ordinary passions of mankind, and, with the two exceptions above mentioned (of celibacy and abstinence in the Order), the doctrine was one of moderation and temperance.

The next Fetter, the fifth, which the converted man has to break is PAṬIGHA, or ill-will. The state of mind here denoted is that which is produced by a consciousness of difference, and is best illustrated by the meditation called the Brahma Vihāra, or "the Highest Condition,"—practised by the early Buddhists to get rid of this sense of difference. It is the Buddha who is represented as speaking:

"And he lets his mind pervade one quarter of the

world with thoughts of love, and so the second, and so the third, and so the fourth. And thus the whole wide world, above, below, around and everywhere, does he continue to pervade with heart of Love, far reaching, grown great, and beyond measure.

"Just, Vāseṭṭha, as a mighty trumpeter makes himself heard, and that without difficulty, towards all the four directions; even so of all things that have shape or form, there is not one that he passes by or leaves aside, but regards them all with mind set free and deep-felt love." *

The exercise is then repeated, substituting each time for Love, first Pity, then Sympathy, and then Equanimity. By this means the strength of the fifth fetter is gradually weakened, and at last destroyed.

To have conquered these two enemies of the higher life lands the "sotāpanno" at the end of the Third Stage, the whole of the Second and Third Stages being occupied with the struggle against them. The path leading immediately to Arahatship is occupied with sundering the last five of these fetters, which one may take together. They are: (6) RŪPARĀGA, the love of life on earth, literally, in the worlds of Form; (7) ARŪPARĀGA, desire for a future

* *Mahā Sudassana Sutta*, ii., 8, and often elsewhere. See my note at *Buddhist Suttas*, p. 201.

life in heaven, literally, in the Formless worlds; (8) MANO, which is Pride; (9) UDDHACCA, or Self-righteousness, and (10) AVIJJĀ, or Ignorance. We find here again that the Buddhist ethics harps once more upon the old question, which crops up so often, of the folly of a craving after a future life. And we ought not to be surprised to find that it is not expected that this inherited desire, which really owes its strength to the great length of time during which it has grown up, should be quite extinguished until nearly the end of the struggle, until victory is nearly won. It is quite characteristic also of the Buddhist faith to find self-righteousness and ignorance placed at the very end of the list, as the last and most difficult enemies which the good Buddhist, in his struggle for self-mastery, has to overcome.

To have acquired, as an habitual frame of mind, the eight positive characteristics laid down in the Noble Path, to have got rid of the ten failings specified in the list of the Fetters, constitutes Arahatship, the Buddhist ideal of life. Directly or indirectly this is the one subject of the earliest Buddhist books. The most eloquent passages lead up to it; the longest (and to us, sometimes I am afraid, the most tedious) deal with the details of it. One might fill pages with the awe-struck and ecstatic praise lavished in the writings of the early Buddhists, men or women, who had reached this state, upon the glorious bliss and peace of the mental condition it involved. They had endless love names for it, each based on one of the phases of the many-sided whole. It is Emancipation, the Island of refuge, the End of craving, the State of purity, the Supreme, the Transcendent, the Uncreate, the Tranquil, the Unchanging, the Going-out, the Unshaken, the Imperishable, the Ambrosia, and so on, in almost endless variety. One of the epithets is very familiar to us in the West; being indeed much more exclusively used by European, than by Buddhist writers, as a name for the Buddhist ideal. This epithet is Nirvana, "the going out"; that is to say, the going out, in the heart, of the three fires of lust, ill-will, and dulness. It is very characteristic that the going out of dulness should be part of the Buddhist salvation. But our hour has come to its close. We have no time left in which to discuss the exact force of each of these epithets, or to attempt, further than has already been possible, to describe the Arahat. We shall have to return to the subject in the next lecture. It must suffice to remind you here that so predominant is this subject in the Buddhist Piṭakas that it is not too much to say that Arahatship is Buddhism. And I will close by quoting (with the alteration of a single word) a poem by an English author, who, while not thinking at all of Buddhism, has managed to convey, in the language of the nineteenth century, the kind of feeling that animated the Arahats of old.

"'T is self whereby we suffer. 'T is the greed
To grasp, the hunger to assimilate
All that earth holds of fair and delicate,
The lust to blend with beauteous lives, to feed
And take our fill of loveliness, which breed
This anguish of the soul intemperate.
'T is self that turns to harm and poisonous hate
The calm clear life of love that Arahats lead.
Oh! that 't were possible this self to burn
In the pure flame of joy contemplative!
Then might we love all loveliness, nor yearn
With tyrannous longings; undisturbed might live
Greeting the summer's and the spring's return,
Nor wailing that their bloom is fugitive." *

* From John Addington Symonds's *Animi Figura* (Eros and Anteros).

LECTURE V.

The Secret of Buddhism.

Part II.—The Wheel of Life and Arahatship.

WE can now, I think, venture on an explanation of the Wheel of Life with which we opened the last lecture. You will recollect that I read you a list of the successive links in the circumference of that wheel, an ancient picture of which has been discovered in Ajanta. It was the discovery of the chain of causation depicted on this wheel, which, in the Vinaya account of the attainment of Buddhahood, is made the essential point of the Buddha's extraordinary insight. And the chain of causation itself is a kind of summary of the way in which the real facts of existence presented themselves to the Buddha's mind. We had yesterday a description of the Noble Eightfold Path, and of the Ten Fetters which the Buddhist has to break. But why should he go along the path? Why should he break the fetters? What is the prison-house in which he is chained up? What is the goal to which he hopes the path will carry him?

The answers to these questions must occupy us to-day. The salvation the Buddhist seeks cannot be accurately described either as a salvation from hell, or as a salvation from sin. The Indian belief in transmigration made the belief in a hell (and for the matter of that, in a heaven, in the Christian sense) impossible. All the beings in all the heavens and hells would necessarily die (as we should say), fall from that state (as the Indians would say), when the causal efficacy of the Karma which put them there had been exhausted. The terrible thing was not a re-birth in hell so much as the far more staggering and terrifying conception that there was no escape from the round of transmigration at all. A being in a state of misery, or in a state of happiness, might be perfectly sure that that state would sooner or later come to an end; but it would come to an end only by the commencement of another state, of another birth. And that birth would be inevitably attended by all the results inherent in the limitations of individuality. And the struggle necessary to keep the individuality alive would bring with it fresh cares and troubles, old age and death, grief, lamentations, wailings, and despair. This is the evil to be avoided.

Arahatship is no doubt an end in itself. It is a state of bliss unspeakable. But it is also an escape from the whirlpool of re-births, and it is as a salvation from that, that it is put forward as the goal to be sought for, the aim to be realised. And the wheel of life is an attempt to describe the real causes which keep men bound in the whirlpool of re-births.

This belief in the whirlpool of re-births was part of the dominant creed at the time when the Buddha worked out his system. The theologies had their theory of escape from it—a theory only made workable by the introduction of a *deus ex machinâ*. The Buddha was bound to give his answer too. It is a kind of necessary *argumentum ad hominem*. But though the doctrine of Arahatship can be considered on its merits, apart from the theory of transmigration, yet the Wheel of Life also is none the less a part, and an important part, of his system.

AVIJJĀ—ignorance—is the first link in the chain of causation. It is the picture of Avijjā which stands hard-by the first spoke in the wheel of life. The symbol in the Ajanta fresco is a blind camel led by a driver. In the Tibetan picture it is simply a blind man feeling his way with a stick. And in the reproduction of a Japanese illustration of the wheel, published last year by Professor Bastian of Berlin, the figure is a demon. In any case, what is meant is, that it is Ignorance which is the cause of Individuality. To attempt to explain what lies behind this enigmatic expression would occupy the rest of my time, nor even then perhaps would the mystery be satisfactorily cleared up. The course of reasoning is analogous to that by which a modern European philosopher seeks to find the explanation of life in the "unconscious will to live"; and you may understand Avijjā, for our present purpose, as a productive unconscious ignorance.

The second link is the SANKHĀRAS, or conformations (literally, Confections). In the Dialogues they are divided into three—thought, word, and deed.* But in the *Abhidhamma* and in the later books, they are divided into fifty-two divisions of thought, word, and deed, and mean practically all those immaterial qualities and capabilities which go to make up the individual. They are represented in the Ajanta fresco, by a potter working at his wheel, surrounded by pots; in the later Tibetan picture, by the wheel and the pots without the potter; and in the still later Japanese picture, by the potter's wheel alone.

It is curious that, as is pointed out by Mr. Waddell, this is precisely the Egyptian symbol of the Creator. It represents no doubt the shaping of the

* See my wife's article in the *Journal R. A. S.*, 1894, p. 325.

crude and formless mental aggregates by the Karma, and an old Sanskrit poem sheds light upon it when it says:

> "Our mind is but a lump of clay
> Which Fate, grim potter, holds
> On sorrow's wheel that rolls alway,
> And, as he pleases, moulds."

The third is VIÑÑĀNA, or Consciousness, represented in the fresco and the Japanese picture by an ape; in the Tibetan counterpart, by an ape climbing a tree. The Tibetan lāmas explain this as showing the rudimentary being becoming anthropoid, but still an unreasoning automaton. I am very doubtful of the validity of this explanation; but there can, I think, be no question that the stage typified is the first rise of consciousness.

The fourth link is NĀMA-RŪPA, or Name and Form, represented on the fresco by two figures, the meaning of which I cannot make out. In the Tibetan picture, it is a boat crossing a stream; and in the Japanese, the same with a man in the boat. The idea is no doubt that of a man crossing the ocean of life. He has now acquired a name and outward form, and has started on an earthly career as a man, endowed with self-consciousness and all the capacities of a sentient individual.*

* That the word "name" should imply mind is due to the pre-Buddhistic use of the word, the result of the superstition that a man's name was a part of his personality.

The fifth is the SAḶ-ĀYATANA, the six "provinces" or "territories," *i. e.*, of the senses: to wit, our five senses and the mind (or mano), regarded as itself an organ of sense. These are represented in the fresco as the mask of a face, with eyes, nose, ears, and mouth, and with blank eye-sockets in the forehead to represent the inner sense or mind. This face is, as it were, "The Empty House of the Senses," and is represented in the Tibetan picture by a house with six windows; and in the Japanese, by the figure of a man.

The sixth link is PHASSO, or Contact, which, in the fresco, is unfortunately missing, but is represented in the Tibetan picture by a man seated with an arrow entering the eye. The idea, no doubt, is, that for a sense-perception to be complete you must have the object-impression from without, as well as the sense-organ to receive the impression.

The seventh link in the chain is VEDANĀ, or Sensation, effaced in the fresco, but represented in both the Tibetan and Japanese pictures by lovers embracing.

Then we have TAṆHĀ, or Thirst, also effaced in the fresco, but represented in the two pictures by a man drinking. That craving should follow from sensation, and sensation from contact, is perfectly simple; and has been well illustrated by Sir Edwin Arnold's lines in *The Light of Asia:*

"Trishṇā, that thirst which makes the living drink
Deeper and deeper and deeper of the false salt waves,
Whereon they float,—pleasures, ambition, wealth,
Praise, fame or domination, conquest, love,
Rich meats and robes and fair abodes and pride
Of ancient lines, and lust of days, and strife
To live, and sins that flow from strife, some sweet,
Some bitter. Thus Life's thirst quenches itself
With draughts which double thirst."*

The ninth link is UPĀDĀNA—literally, Grasping—represented in the Tibetan picture by a man picking flowers. It typifies the attachment to worldly things which the human being ignorantly grasps at, supposing they will quench this craving thirst which has arisen from sensation.

Now the tenth link is BHAVA, literally, "Becoming," the tendency to be. This idea, the symbol for which is effaced in the fresco and indistinct in the Japanese, is represented in the Tibetan picture by a pregnant woman; and the eleventh link—JĀTI, Birth,—is represented by the birth of a child. The idea, no doubt, is that it is the grasping disposition which leads to re-birth. So Plato in his simile of re-birth (in the *Phaedo*) represents the soul, which should rise to heaven, as dragged down into re-existence by the steed Epithumia, that is, craving or appetite; and he explains this by saying: "Through craving

* *Light of Asia*, p. 165.

after the corporeal, which never leaves them, they are imprisoned finally in another body," etc. He then goes on to give examples, and winds up with the absolutely Indian saying, that "He who is a philosopher, or lover of learning, and is entirely pure at departing, is alone permitted to attain to the divine nature." As I have quoted the whole passage, together with its context, in my *Hibbert Lectures*, pp. 95–98, I will only remind you here of this curious coincidence between Eastern and Western thought.

The twelfth and last link in the chain of causation is simply the inevitable result of the eleventh—the old age, decay, and death, with the accompanying grief, which follow upon each new birth.

The whole picture of this wheel or chain of causation seems to me to be an attempt at expressing what happens in every human life. I do not think that each separate link is necessarily intended to follow the preceding one in time. It is not intended, *e.g.*, that link No. 3 is necessarily posterior in time to link No. 2. There is a dependence of each one of these links upon the other, but the dependence is not always of the same kind, either of time or of cause and effect. This has been well pointed out by Mr. H. C. Warren of Cambridge, Mass., in a very suggestive article in the *Journal of the American Oriental Society* for 1893. But the interpretation of the wheel is not yet, to my mind, entirely satisfactory. The text only lies at present before us in the extremely curt phraseology of the passage I have read; and no commentary upon it is as yet accessible. And even when we have the help of further passages in the Pali, the whole subject will have to be studied by someone more intimately acquainted with the history of philosophic conceptions than I can claim to be. My wife has pointed out, in the *Journal of the Royal Asiatic Society* for 1894 (p. 388), that, in the Orphic theogony, we come across the notion of re-birth considered as a weary unending circle of birth, a wheel of fate (κύκλος τῆς γενέσεως, ὁ τῆς μοίρας τροχός). From this wheel the soul longs to escape, and entreats the gods, especially Dionysos, for release from the wheel. Again, in the verses inscribed on one of the three golden funereal tablets dug up near the site of Sybaris, it is said, "And thus I escape from the cycle, the misery-laden."

Pindar, Empedokles, and Plato, as is well known, all entertained the notion of repeated re-birth in this world, which, according to the later writers, often included in its phases incarnation as an animal or even as a vegetable. It is possible that all three derived this notion from Pythagoras, and throughout there runs the Orphic (and also the Buddhist) idea of each re-birth being a stage in a course of moral evolution and effort after purification. Empedokles, however, sees not a wheel, but rather a toilsome road or roads of life. Professor Garbe, in his book which I quoted in the first lecture, the just published *Sānkhya Philosophie*, repeats his opinion expressed in the *Monist* of January, 1894, that the Greeks did actually borrow, in other respects, from the Indian philosophers. And Professor von Schroeder, in his treatise *Pythagoras und die Inder*, seems to me to have quite clearly made out his case in favour of a borrowing by Pythagoras. It is at least certain that the students of ancient philosophy will do well to study more carefully than hitherto the Indian parallels; and I hope I shall therefore be excused for having turned aside, in this connection, to notice a few of the most interesting.

What is at least certain is that the Buddhist, like the Vedāntist, the Sānkhya, and the Greek views just referred to (as well as in the Keltic parallels quoted in my *Hibbert Lectures*, pp. 76, 77), looked upon salvation, not as an escape from sin or hell, but from this unending, hopeless wheel of life, on which the ordinary man was being relentlessly whirled round. All the Indian philosophies unite in supposing ignorance to be the origin of the whole evil, the great enemy to be conquered. But they differ in their view as to what the destruction of this ignorance will bring about. According to the Vedāntist, an insight into the pregnant fact that the soul of man is identical with the great soul, the First Cause of all, will lead to a union between God and the "soul," which has only been temporarily interrupted or obscured by the conditions of individuality. So Plato, as we have seen, says that it is only the philosopher, entirely pure at departing, who is permitted to attain to the divine nature.

Buddhism has gone a step beyond this. It holds also that that destruction of ignorance is the way of escape from the wheel of life, but the escape is not reached, and, of course, in the Buddhist system, could not be reached, in a union with God to be attained only in an after-life. The victory to be gained by the destruction of ignorance is, in Gotama's view, a victory which can be gained and enjoyed in this life, and in this life only. This is what is meant by the Buddhist ideal of Arahatship—the life of a man made perfect by insight, the life of a man who has travelled along the "Noble eightfold path" and broken all the "Fetters," and carried out in its entirety, the Buddhist system of self-culture and self-control. The Christian analogue to this state of mind (which, in English books on Buddhism, is usually called Nirvana), is the advent of the Kingdom of Heaven within a man, the "peace that passeth understanding."

As I have reminded you in the last lecture the meaning of the phrase Nirvana, is literally the "going out"; and it is used, in its primary sense, of the going out of the flame of a lamp. In its secondary ethical sense it signifies (*not*, of course, the going out of a "soul," nor the going out of life), but the going out of the threefold fire of lust, ill-will, and delusion or dulness or stupidity. But it involves the going out also of that "Upādāna" or grasping, which would lead to the formation, in another birth, of a new individual. This point is dealt with at greater length in my manual, *Buddhism*, pp. 110–115, where (already in 1877) this view of the real meaning of Nirvana, since confirmed by the publication of the texts, was first put forth.

This then is Buddha's reply to those of his contemporaries who were concerned above all things in escaping from the whirlpool of re-births. "Arahatship will save you: you can save yourselves by Arahatship."

We find a precisely similar state of things when, in the Tevijja Sutta,* the two young Brahmins

* Translated in my *Dialogues of the Buddha*, I., 298–320.

come to him and ask him to shew them the way to a union with God, with Brahmā. "Very well," says the reformer, "I will shew you." And he gives a long exposition of Arahatship. "That is the way."

In both cases the exposition of Arahatship is clear enough. The obscurities begin with the reasoning which endeavours to adapt so untheological a position to a solution of difficulties really based on the current theologies. It is all very well to complain how much easier it would have been simply to deny the facts (the facts of the whirlpool of re-births, and the union with God) rather than to attempt to reconcile them with the new doctrine of Arahatship. But that course of action could have led to only one result. Buddhism would have died in its birth. In any case Gotama adopted the opportunist position, and seems to have thought the reconciliation both clear and complete. And though it is, in my opinion, neither the one nor the other in our present state of knowledge, it is surely wiser to suspend our judgment as to the logical adequacy of the reasonings put forth till the publication of the other half of the texts shall have put us in possession of all the materials on which a judgment should really be formed.

What we have at present ascertained is that, in both cases, Arahatship is the Buddhist solution of the puzzle put. Now as to what constitutes Arahatship we had, in the last lecture, descriptive lists, and discussions of their details. It will be advisable, on this central and most important point of Buddhism, to quote more fully the actual words of the early Buddhist writers.

The Buddhist poems reach their highest level of beauty when they attempt to describe the glory of this state of victory over the world, and over birth and death, of an inward peace that can never be shaken, of a joy that can never be ruffled. Thus, when Kassapa, a distinguished Brahmin teacher, had left all to join the new leader, and the people were astonished at it, he is asked, in the presence of the multitude, to explain the nature of the change that has come over him:

> What hast thou seen, O thou of Uruvelā,
> That thou, for penances so far renowned,
> Forsakest thus thy sacrificial fire?
> I ask thee, Kassapa, the meaning of this thing.
> How comes it that thine altar lies deserted?
> What is it, in the world of men or gods,
> That thy heart longs for? Tell me that, Kassapa!"

And the convert answers:

> "That state of peace I saw, wherein the roots
> Of ever fresh re-birth are all destroyed, and greed
> And hatred and delusion all have ceased,

That state from lust for future life set free,
That changeth not, can ne'er be led to change.
My mind saw that! What care I for those rites?"*

The following two poems are taken from the Sutta Nipāta, from the same collection that contained the ballad, already quoted above, about the first meeting of Gotama and King Bimbisāra.

Dhaniya Sutta.

1. Hot steams my food. My cows are milked.
—So said the herdsman Dhaniya—
Along the banks of the Mahī
With equals and with friends I dwell.
Right well is my trim cottage thatched,
And on my hearth the fire burns bright.
So let the rain pour down now, if it likes, to-night!

2. Cool is my mind. No fallow land lies there.†
—So said the Exalted One—
For one night only, as I wander on,
I dwell upon the banks of the Mahī.
My lodging 's open to the sky. The fires
Are out (for in my heart the flames
Of Lust, Ill-will, and Dulness burn no more).
So let the rain pour down now, if it likes, to-night!

3. There are no gadflies here. My kine
—So said the herdsman Dhaniya—

* *Mahā Vagga* i., 22, 4.

† On the five fallow lands of the mind see *Majjhima Nikāya*, i., 101.

Are roaming thro' the meadows rich with grass ;
Well can they bear the fickle rain god's blows.
So let the rain pour down now, if it likes, to-night !

4. My basket raft was woven well together
—So said the Exalted One—
Crossed over now, I 've reached the farther bank
And overcome the floods (the Lust of Sense
The Lust of Life, Delusion, Ignorance).
So let the rain pour down now, if it likes, to-night !

5. Obedient is my wife, no wanton she,
—So said the herdsman Dhaniya—
Long has she dwelt with me, my well beloved,
I hear no evil thing in her against me.
So let the rain pour down now, if it likes, to-night !

6. Obedient is my heart, wholly set free,
—So said the Exalted One—
Long has it been watched over, well subdued,
No evil thing is found within my breast.
So let the rain pour down now, if it likes, to-night !

7. On my own earnings do I live at ease.
—So said the herdsman Dhaniya—
My boys are all about me, strong in health,
I hear no evil thing in them against me.
So let the rain pour down now, if it likes, to-night !

8. No man can call me servant, and I wander
—So said the Exalted One—
At will, o'er all the earth, on what I find.
I feel no need of wages, or of gain.
So let the rain pour down now, if it likes, to-night !

9. I 've barren cows and sucking calves,
—So said the herdsman Dhaniya—
And cows in calf, and heifers sleek,
And a strong bull, lord o'er the cows.
So let the rain pour down now, if it likes, to-night!

10. No barren cows have I, nor sucking calves,
—So said the Exalted One—
No cows in calf, nor heifers sleek,
Nor a strong bull, lord o'er the cows.
So let the rain pour down now, if it likes, to-night!

11. The stakes are driven in, nothing can shake them,
—So said the herdsman Dhaniya—
The ropes of Muñja grass are new and strong,
No calves could break them loose, and stray.
So let the rain pour down now, if it likes, to-night!

12. I 've broken all the bonds loose, like a bull,
Or like the lordly elephant, calm in his strength,
Contemning the weak strands of jungle rope.
I ne'er again shall enter the dark womb.
So let the rain pour down now, if it likes, to-night!

13. Then lo! a thunder-cloud, filling the hollows,
And the high ground, that moment poured forth rain,
And Dhaniya the herdsman, as he heard
The god's rain rushing, yielded him, and said;

14. O, great the gain that has accrued to us,
In that we met the Exalted One to-day!
In thee of the seeing eye we put our trust.
Be thou, O mighty Sage, a teacher to us.
My wife and I will be obedient;

Under the Happy One we both will lead
A holy life, and pass beyond old age and death,
And put an end, for aye, to every pain!

15. The man with sons takes pride in sons,
—So said Māra, the Evil One—
The man with kine takes joy in kine.
Lusts, evil, and Karma bring delights to men;
He, who has none of these, has no delights.

16. He, who has sons, has sorrow in his sons,
—So said the Exalted One—
He, who has kine, has trouble with his kine.
Lusts, evil, and Karma are the source of care;
He, who has none of these, is not careworn.

Dhaniya Sutta is ended.

Uṭṭhāna Sutta.

1. Rise! sit up! what is the use of sleeping?
How can sleep wait upon the sick at heart?
Upon sick men pierced with the dart of care,
In whose sad heart the dart is rankling still?*

2. Rouse yourselves then, sit up! and steadfastly
Train yourselves, learn, for the sweet sake of peace!
Let not the King of Death, knowing you indolent
Befool you, fallen into his deadly power!

3. That clinging bond in which both gods and men,
Craving with wants, stand caught,—O, conquer that!
Let not the moment pass! For those who let
The moment pass them, mourn in states of woe?†

* See Jātaka, i., 369.

† The two last lines of this verse recur at Thera Gāthā, 404, and at Therī Gāthā, 5.

4. Carelessness is dust and dirt, and carelessness
On carelessness heaped up, defiles the mind.
By earnestness and wisdom let the wise
Draw out the dart that rankles in his heart. *

Uṭṭhāna Sutta is ended.

Here is a passage descriptive of the bliss of the Nirvana of Arahatship:

"Let us live happily then, free from hatred among the hating! Among men who hate let *us* dwell free from ill-will!

"Let us live happily then, free from ailments among the ailing! Among men sick at heart let us dwell free from repining!

"Let us live happily then, free from care among the careworn! Among men devoured by eagerness let us be free from excitement!

"Let us live happily then, we who have no hindrances! We shall be like the bright gods who feed upon happiness!" †

In a later prose description of the kind of feelings that lead a man to seek after Nirvana, we find the words—it is King Milinda who is speaking to Nāgasena the Buddhist—

* This verse is attributed to the son of the Mālunkya woman in the Thera Gāthā, 404.

† Dhamma Pada, verses 197–200.

"Venerable Nāgasena, your people say: 'Nirvana is not past, nor future, nor present, nor produced, nor not produced, nor produceable.' In that case, Nāgasena, does the man who, having ordered his life aright, realise Nirvana, realise something already produced, or does he himself produce it first, and then realise it?"

"Neither the one, O King, nor the other. And, nevertheless, O King, that essence of Nirvana which he, so ordering his life aright, realises—that exists."

"Do not, venerable Nāgasena, clear up this puzzle by making it dark! Make it open and plain as you elucidate it. With a will, strenuous in endeavour, pour out upon it all that has been taught you. It is a point on which this people is bewildered, plunged in perplexity, lost in doubt. Dissipate this guilty uncertainty; it pierces like a dart."

"That principle of Nirvana, O King, so peaceful, so blissful, so delicate, exists. And it is that which he who orders his life aright, grasping the idea of things according to the teachings of the Conquerors, realises by his wisdom—even as a pupil, by his knowledge, makes himself, according to the instruction of his teacher, master of an art.

"And if you ask: 'How is Nirvana to be known?' it is by freedom from distress and danger, by confidence, by peace, by calm, by bliss, by happiness, by delicacy, by purity, by freshness. . . .

"And if again you should ask: 'How does he who orders his life aright realise that Nirvana?' I should reply: 'He, O King, who orders his life aright grasps the truth as to the development of all things, and when he is doing so he perceives therein birth, he perceives old age, he perceives disease, he perceives death. But he perceives not therein, whether in the beginning or the middle or the end, anything worthy of being laid hold of as lasting satisfaction . . . And discontent arises in his mind when he thus finds nothing fit to be relied on as lasting satisfaction, and a fever takes possession of his body, and without a refuge or protection, hopeless, he becomes weary of repeated lives. . . . And in the mind of him who thus perceives the insecurity of transitory life, of starting afresh in innumerable births, the thought arises: 'All on fire is this endless becoming, burning and blazing! Full of pain is it, of despair! If only one could reach a state in which there were no becoming, *there* would there be calm, *that* would be sweet —the cessation of all these conditions, the getting rid of all these defects (of lusts, of evil, and of Karma), the end of cravings, the absence of passion, peace, Nirvana!'

"And therewith does his mind leap forward into that state in which there is no becoming, and then has he found peace, then does he exult and rejoice at the thought: 'A refuge have I gained at last!' Just, O King, as a man who, venturing into a strange land, has lost his way, on becoming aware of a path, free from jungle, that will lead him home, bounds forward along it, contented in mind, exulting and rejoicing at the thought: 'I have found the way at last!'—Just so in him who thus perceives the insecurity of transitory births there arises the thought: 'All on fire is this endless becoming, burning and blazing! Full of pain is it and despair! If only one could reach a state in which there were no becoming, *there* would there be calm, *that* would be sweet—the cessation of all these conditions, the getting rid of all these defects, the end of craving, the absence of passion, peace, Nirvana!' And therewith does his mind leap forward into that state in which there is no becoming, and then has he found peace, then does he exult and rejoice at the thought: 'A refuge have I found at last!' And he strives with might and main along that path, searches it out, accustoms himself thoroughly to it; to that end does he make firm his self-possession, to that end does he hold fast in effort, to that end does he remain steadfast in love toward all beings in all the worlds; and still to that does he direct his mind again and again, until, gone far beyond the transitory, he gains the Real, the highest fruit of Arahatship. And when he has gained that, O King, the man who has ordered his life aright has realised, seen face to face, Nirvana!" *

Then after this discussion as to the time at which, and the manner by which, Nirvana can be obtained, the author goes on to discuss where Nirvana is stored up. The answer is that there is no such place, and the discussion then goes on:

"Venerable Nāgasena, let it be granted that there is no place where Nirvana is stored up. But is there any place on which a man may stand and, by ordering his life aright, realise Nirvana?"

"Yes, O King, there is such a place."

"Which, then, Nāgasena, is that place?"

"Virtue, O King, is the place. For if grounded in virtue, and careful in attention—whether in the land of the Skythians or the Greeks, whether in China or in Tartary, whether in Alexandria or Nikumba, whether in Benares or in Kosala, whether in Kashmir or in Gandhāra, whether on a mountain top or in the highest heavens—wheresoever he may be, the man who orders his life aright will attain Nirvana." †

* *Questions of King Milinda*, vol. ii., pp. 195-201.

† *Questions of King Milinda*, pp. 202-204.

We have several descriptions in the older books of the man who has actually attained this Nirvana of Arahatship. But there are none of them, so far as I know, that purport to contain the whole description. Perhaps we may find this in the Visuddhi Magga, or *Path of Purity*, now being edited and translated by Mr. Henry C. Warren of Cambridge, Mass. We have a more complete characterisation of the ideal Buddhist Recluse (which comes to much the same thing) in a work later than the Canon:

"Just, O King, as a lotus flower of glorious, pure, and high descent and origin is glossy, soft, desirable, sweet-smelling, longed for, loved, and praised, untarnished by the water or the mud, graced with tiny petals and filaments and pericarps, the resort of many bees, a child of the clear, cold stream, just so is that disciple of the Noble Ones endowed with the thirty Graces. And what are the thirty?

"1. His heart is full of affectionate, soft, and tender love.

"2. Evil is killed, destroyed, cast out from within him.

"3 and 4. Pride and self-righteousness are put an end to and cast down.

"5. Stable and strong and established and undeviating is his self-confidence.

"6. He enters into the enjoyment of the heart's refreshment, the highly praised and desirable peace and bliss of the ecstasies of contemplation fully felt.

"7. He exhales the most excellent and unequalled sweet savour of righteousness of life.

"8. Near is he and dear to gods and men alike.

"9. Exalted by the best of beings, the Arahat Noble Ones themselves.

"10. Gods and men delight to honour him.

"11. The enlightened, wise, and learned approve, esteem, and appreciate him.

"12. Untarnished is he by the love either of this world or the next.

"13. He sees the danger in the smallest, most insignificant offence.

"14. Rich is he in the best of wealth—the wealth that is the fruit of the Path, the wealth of those who are seeking the highest of the Attainments.

"15. He is in receipt, in full measure, of the four requisites of a recluse (food, lodging, clothing, and medicine).

"16. He lives without a home, addicted to that best austerity that is dependent on meditation.

"17. He has unravelled the whole net of evil. He has broken and burst through, doubled up and utterly destroyed, the possibility of re-birth in any of the five future states.

"18. He has broken and burst through the five obstacles to the highest life in this world (lust, malice, sloth, pride, and doubt).

"19. He is unalterable in character.

"20. He is excellent in conduct.

"21. He transgresses none of the rules as to the four requisites of a recluse.

"22. He has passed beyond all perplexity.

"23. His mind is set upon complete emancipation.

"24. He has seen the truth.

"25. The sure and steadfast place of refuge from all fear has he gained.

"26. The seven evil inclinations (to lust, and malice, and heresy, and doubt, and pride, and desire for future life, and ignorance) are rooted out in him.

"27. He has reached the end of the Great Evils (lust, future life, delusion, and ignorance).

"28, 29. He abounds in peace, and the bliss of the ecstasies of contemplation.

"30. He is endowed with all the virtues a recluse should have.

"These, O King, are the thirty Graces he is adorned withal." *

I might go on quoting such passages, but they

* *Questions of King Milinda*, ii., pp. 271–273.

would weary you, and I must find time to mention the thirty-seven constituent elements of Arahatship.

The word itself means "the-state-of-one-who-is-worthy," or "noble," and this state of mind is divided, in the oldest books, into these thirty-seven constituent parts. They are called the Medicines Discovered by the Great Physician.*

"Of all the medicines found in all the world,
Many in number, various in their powers,
Not one equals this medicine of the Truth.
Drink that, O brethren. Drink, and drinking,—live!

"For having drunk that medicine of the Truth,
Ye shall have passed beyond old age, and death
And—evil, lusts, and Karma rooted out—
Thoughtful and seeing, ye shall be at rest!"

Or, to put it in another way: Just before Gotama died, he is said † to have convened a special meeting of the Order, and to have said:

"Which then, O Brethren, are the dispositions which, when I had perceived, I made known to you; which, when you have mastered, it behoves you to practise, meditate upon, and spread abroad, in order that pure religion may last long and be perpetuated,

* *Milinda*, ii., 218.

† In the *Mahā Parinibbāna Sutta*, translated in my *Buddhist Suttas*, p. 6.

in order that it may continue to be for the good and happiness of the great multitude, out of pity for the world, to the good and the gain and the weal of gods and men? They are these:

The Four Earnest Meditations.
The Fourfold Great Struggle against Error.
The Four Roads to Saintship.
The Five Moral Powers.
The Five Organs of Spiritual Sense.
The Seven Kinds of Wisdom, and
The Noble Eightfold Path.

"Behold, now, O Brethren, I exhort you, saying:

"All component things must grow old. Work out your salvation with diligence. The final passing away of the Tathāgata will take place before long. At the end of three months from this time the Tathāgata will die.

"My age is now full ripe; my life draws to its close.
I leave you, I depart, relying on myself alone.
Be earnest then, O brethren, active, full of thought;
Be steadfast in resolve! Keep watch over your own hearts.
Who wearies not, but holds fast to this truth and law,
Shall cross this sea of life, shall make an end of grief!"*

Now I very deeply regret that, being obliged to

* *Book of the Great Decease*, iii., 65, translated in my *Buddhist Suttas*, pp. 62, 63.

put the whole of the higher Buddhism into two lectures, I am precluded from dealing at any length with any of the above thirty-seven details. I am painfully aware how uninteresting such bare lists are apt to be, when the full meaning implied by the pregnant terms enumerated is not completely brought out and illustrated by examples drawn from similar systems in the West. But I have endeavoured, so far as in me lies, to bring out, in what I have already said, the essential points of the deeper view of life which lies behind all Buddhism; and I can only venture to trouble you now with a few general remarks on this system of ethical discipline.

And first I would observe that the whole system is based on intellectual activity. It is no doubt often related in the Buddhist books, and must often have happened, that an eloquent address on the impermanence of all things, on the delusions of self, on the vanity of earthly things (wealth, power, and renown), will have led to the conversion of some hearer whose personal experience had prepared him for the reception of the truth. But though, in that way, a hearer may, in the eloquent words of the passage I have read you from the *Milinda*, have leaped forward along the way and arrived by a sudden flash of insight at some, even advanced, stage of the Noble Path; still it was required of him to keep up a constant intellectual activity in order to hold fast what he had attained, and reach out to further things beyond.

Secondly, it is throughout regarded that wrong belief, the nursing of delusions, the dulness which cannot open its eyes to the deep realities of life, are in themselves ethically wrong; that to believe a lie is an obstacle to any advance along the path, and that the Arahat has to be constantly steadfast and earnest in keeping his views whole and sound.

Thirdly, that it is the greatest mistake to suppose that the suppression of desire is a part of the higher Buddhism. It is really just the contrary. Evil desires are, no doubt, to be suppressed. It is true that some of the desires which in modern Western life are held to be natural, and worthy of satisfaction, such as the desire for a wife and family, for wealth and power and titles, are, in Arahatship, regarded as obstacles to the attainment of the goal. But to the Buddhist layman the satisfaction of these desires is freely permitted and even regulated by precept; and it is at least an open question whether we could not match every expression as to the suppression of such desires with equivalents from the teachings of Western prophets. Even with regard to the sexual relations Gotama finds himself in agreement with many earnest Christian writers. It is at all events certain, that the ideal is not one of mere quietism, but of intellectual activity and of exalted desire, not only entertained, but reached and enjoyed. "Entering the Order did not mean," as my wife has said in the article already quoted, "mere mortification of feeling or deadening of energies. It was a diversion of both into new channels. The Arahats are as exalted and virtually as hedonistic in their aspirations as any Christian saint. Of them too, Matthew Arnold could have said:

> "Ye like angels appear
> Radiant with ardour divine,
> Beacons of hope ye appear,
> Languor is not in your heart,
> Weakness is not in your work,
> Weariness not on your brow."

The fourth point is the joyousness of the Arahat, springing more especially from the emancipation of heart to which he has attained, and on which so much stress is laid. Thus, in the Mahāparinibbāna Sutta (a few pages after Gotama, on the eve of his decease, has insisted on his disciples being a lamp unto themselves), the Blessed One says:

"It is through not understanding and grasping four conditions, O Brethren, that we have had to run so long, to wander so long, in this weary path of transmigration—both you and I. And what are these four? When noble conduct is realised and known, and noble meditation and noble wisdom, and noble freedom, is realised and known, then is the craving for becoming rooted out, that which leads to renewed life is destroyed, and there is no more birth.

Righteousness, earnest thought, wisdom and freedom sublime,
These are the truths realised by Gotama far-renowned.
Knowing them, he the knower, proclaimed the truth to the brethren;
The Master with eye divine, the quencher of grief must die." *

The emancipation of heart is one of the "Seven Jewels" of the Blessed One, and describing it, the author of the *Milinda* says: †

"There is one diadem that is the chief of all, and that is this diadem of Emancipation of heart!

"All the people that dwell in a house look up
To their Lord when he wears his crown of gems—
The wide world of the gods and of men looks up
To the wearer of Freedom's diadem!"

It was the "gentle liberty" of a higher, wider law by which to regulate and concentrate their lives, that all those who had realised the doctrine of impermanence were to strive after. The emancipation was no doubt an emancipation from delusions; the freedom did not extend to license to revert to the

* *Book of the Great Decease*, iv., 2. † *Milinda* ii., p. 224.

errors which they had renounced, or to embrace, in intellectual anarchism, any analogous errors in their ethical development. But within those limits, which must have been clear to you from the earlier part of this lecture, there was perfect freedom from dogma, perfect liberty of thought.

But I am not concerned to defend the accuracy, or the completeness, or the adequacy of the solution put forward by Gotama of the problem of practical ethics. It is true that in my humble opinion no historian can be an adequate historian without sympathy, and indeed I confess I should not have devoted my life to the study of Buddhism, had I not felt the intrinsic worth of much that Gotama laid down. And it is at least interesting to remember that Gotama was the only man of our own race, the only Aryan, who can rank as the founder of a great religion. Not only so, but the whole intellectual and religious development of which Buddhism is the final outcome was distinctively Aryan, and Buddhism is the one essentially Aryan faith.

But we do not need to go back 2500 years to seek for truth. We have to fight out the problem of ethics for ourselves and for our own times. The point I stand here to submit to your consideration, is that the study of ethics, and especially the study of ethical theory in the West, has hitherto resulted in a deplorable failure through irreconcilable logomachies and the barrenness of speculation cut off from actual fact. The only true method of ethical inquiry is surely the historical method. As the President of Cornell University in his "Ethical Import of Darwinism" has so ably put it:

"How is ethics as a science possible? If it is ever to rise above the analytic procedure of logic, it can only be by becoming one of the historical sciences. Given the earliest morality of which we have any written record, to trace from it, through progressive stages, the morality of to-day—*that* is the problem, and the only problem, which can fall within the scope of a truly scientific ethic. The discovery of these historical sequences constitutes the peculiarity of the science, which, like every other, pre-supposes observation, analysis, and classification."

Surely this is the sound gospel, and I cannot be wrong in maintaining that the study of Buddhism should be considered a necessary part of any ethical course, and should not be dismissed in a page or two, but receive its due proportion in the historical perspective of ethical evolution. I venture to appeal, therefore, in conclusion, to the friends of higher education in America, to recognise the importance of finding a place in their curriculum for the proper treatment of this most interesting and suggestive study.

LECTURE VI.

Some Notes on the History of Buddhism.

ANY presentation of Buddhism would be very imperfect without at least an attempt to sketch the most instructive and suggestive history of the curious developments which, during its long career, it has, in different times and places, undergone. This history is especially interesting from a comparative point of view. Buddhism starts with a complete philosophical and psychological theory worked out by men of great intellectual power and considerable culture. It took its rise among an advancing and conquering people full of pride in their colour and their race, in their achievements and their progress. It advocated a view in many respects far in advance of what had been reached and, for the matter of that, of what has even now been reached by the average philosophic and religious mind. It made its first conquests in a great continent occupied by peoples of various races and holding widely different views; their leaders often, it is true, well trained in philosophic thought, but the mass of the folk entangled in multiform varieties of an indiscriminating animism. And it soon spread over the frontiers among nations, some of them more barbarous still than the then most uncultured Indians. Buddhism has been adopted by the wild hordes on the cold table-lands of Nepal, Tartary, and Tibet, by the cultured Chinese in their varying climes, in the peninsula of Korea, whence it spread to the islands of Japan, and by the Sinhalese and Siamese under the palm groves of the south. It has penetrated on the west to the confines of Europe; on the north it numbers its adherents amid the snow and ice of Siberia; and in the far east it was the dominant religion for centuries in the beautiful islands of the Javanese archipelago. Wherever it has gone it has been so modified by the national characteristics and the inherited beliefs of its converts, acting upon the natural tendencies within itself to alteration and decay, that it has developed, under these conditions, into strangely inconsistent and even antagonistic beliefs and practices. But each of these beliefs breathes more or less of the spirit of the system out of which they all alike have grown, and most interesting it is to trace the causes which have produced out of it such different results.

It would be premature to attempt, in our present state of knowledge, to trace any development in doctrine in the sacred books themselves. Except in one particular, the system presented to our view in the dialogues, as repeated in the Anguttara and Samyutta Nikāyas, as developed in the psychological books, and as used as the basis of the poetry, presents the picture of a continuous and consistent whole. And this is not surprising considering the perfection of the system as it came from the hands of the Master, and the intellectual activity, and enthusiastic culture, of the men by whom it was first handed down. But in the century or two after the death of Gotama, during which the books, as we have them, were put into their present shape, there was time enough for a very considerable growth of opinion concerning the person of their revered teacher.

Most of these developments were due to the later books after the canon was closed. The various details referred to in Lecture III., in which the later accounts of the Jātaka, and of the Sanskrit poems, have been anticipated in an unpublished Suttanta, relate only to the legend of his birth.* And even on this matter the later versions are, as one would expect, much more expanded.

* *Journ. R. A. S.*, 1894, pp. 386, 387.

But the first disruption in the Order took place on other questions, namely, on matters connected with the regulation of the Order itself. One hundred years after the death of Buddha, according to the oldest account preserved in an appendix to the *Khandakas*, there arose a certain party in the Order which proclaimed and practised a loosening of the rules in ten particulars. These ten particulars seem to us now to be very trumpery; just as the disputes between the Irish and Romish sections of the Christian Church at the synod of Whitby, held in the seventh century, seem to us moderns to be concerning matters of little moment,—the exact position and shape of the tonsure and the exact dating of the Easter festival. No doubt in both cases there were greater differences behind, and though these are not apparent in the most ancient Buddhist account they come out very strongly in later writers. As I have given the whole list of the ten indulgences in my manual, *Buddhism*, I need not repeat them here; and will only remind you that the last and most important of them was, that gold and silver might be received by members of the Order.

To put an end to the disputes upon these points a Council of the leading members of the Order was held at Vesāli and the heretical opinions were condemned. The long-continued struggle on the question—as important for the history of Buddhism as the Arian controversy for that of Christianity—agitated the whole Buddhist world to its very centre. And the decision on the point, given at this Council of Vesāli, led to a serious schism in the Buddhist Church.

Now the ten indulgences are each summed up in a single word; and these words are, each and all of them, conspicuous by their absence from the books on the laws and regulations of the Order included in the canon, except that they appear in an historical account added, quite evidently as an appendix, to the collection of treatises, or *Khandakas*, described in my second lecture. This fact is of the very greatest importance in determining the date at which those *Khandakas* must have been composed. The ten points in dispute were all matters of ecclesiastical law. They all related to observances of the Brotherhood. Is it probable that, in a set of rules and treatises which seek to set forth, down to the minutest detail, and even with hair-splitting diffuseness, all that has any relation to the daily life of the Brethren and the regulation of the Buddhist Order, —is it probable that, in such a collection, if, when it was compiled, the struggle on these ten points had already burst into flame, there should be no reference at all, even in interpolations, to any one of these ten disputes? That the difference of opinion on each of the ten points remains altogether unnoticed in that part of the rules and treatises where, in the natural order of things, it would be obviously referred to—that the rules are not in any way altered to cover, or to suggest, any decision of the points in dispute,—and that they are only mentioned in an appendix where the Council held to decide them is described, shows clearly that the rules and treatises, as we have them, must have been put together before the time when the Council of Vesāli was held.*

The ancient story of the Council stops at the point where the ten indulgences are rejected. But the Ceylon chronicles, which have preserved the tradition of the orthodox school (and are therefore, notwithstanding their later date, very good evidence as *against* that school), admit that the matter did not rest there. They say that the adherents of the ten indulgences proceeded to hold a council of their own, and I will read you the account of what they admit that the heretics did. The animus of the description only entitles it to a greater confidence.

The Dīpa Vansa, the older of the two Chronicles in question, has the following words: †

* The above argument is taken from the Introd. to *Vinaya Texts from the Pali*, pp. xxi., xxii.

† Book v., verses 32 and following.

"The monks of the Great Council twisted the teaching round.
They broke up the original scriptures and made a new recension,
A chapter put in one place they put in another,
And distorted the sense and the doctrine of the Five Nikāyas.
These monks—who knew neither what had been spoken at length
Nor what had been spoken in abstract, neither
What was the obvious nor what the higher meaning—
Put things referring to one matter as if they referred to another,
And destroyed much of the spirit by holding to the shadow of the letter.
They partly rejected the Sutta, and the Vinaya so deep,
And made another rival Sutta and Vinaya of their own.
The Parivāra abstract, and the book of the Abhidhamma,
The Paṭisambhidā, the Niddesa, and a portion of the Jātaka,
So much they put aside, and made others in their place.
They rejected the well known rules of nouns and genders too,
Of composition and of literary skill, and put others in their place."

This council of the heretics we see was called, as the orthodox chroniclers admit, "The Great Council," which seems to show that the number of its adherents was not to be despised; and from it, in the next two centuries and a half, seventeen bodies of more or less heretical doctrine were gradually formed in the Buddhist Church. These were not sects in our sense. There was no division of organisation, or church government. There were no such things as churches, or church services; and the divisions, such as they were, remained solely differences of opinion. Various schools were named, for the most part, after the names of some great teachers, or after the locality in which they took their rise. Only a few of the names refer to matters of doctrine. The division did not therefore correspond to the division between Greek Catholics, Roman Catholics, Episcopalians, Independents, and so forth, but rather to the division between Broad, High, and Low Church. We have, unfortunately, none of their early books surviving. It would appear, from the passage just read from the Dīpa Vansa, that all the schools continued to use the books in the Piṭakas, though they made changes in some of them. For the only books which they are stated to have rejected are those of the Abhidhamma, and three prose works included in the Appendix described to you in my second lecture, and one other, the Parivāra, or student's manual, which has been added to the canon law, that is to the Rules and the Treatises.

The canon law itself was in fact retained, subject no doubt to slight alterations and differences of interpretation. So also it is not stated that they rejected any of the Dialogues, or even the great rearrangements of Buddhist doctrine in the Anguttara and Saṃyutta Nikāyas.

It is scarcely credible that, had they done so, it would not have been thrown in their teeth by the orthodox chroniclers and commentators; and it is expressly implied that they accepted, and continued to use, all the books of religious and philosophical poetry. Even as late as the time of Asoka we find that Tissa, the son of Moggalī, the author of the Kathā Vatthu, in his arguments against those who differed from the orthodox school, appeals throughout to the Piṭaka texts, and takes it for granted that his opponents will acknowledge them as decisive. But no doubt the leaders of the various schools did, from time to time, compile works now lost, but of which we may some day be able to gather some fragments from Sanskrit, Tibetan, and Chinese manuscripts still extant, though not translated.

As to the actual points at issue, the best authority is, of course, the Kathā Vatthu itself. The author states the various theses put forward by his opponents, but does not specify who they are, nor to what school they belong. This information is afforded to us by the Commentary on the Kathā Vatthu, which has been edited in full for the Pali Text Society, although it has not been translated. This traditional interpretation and identification of the schools referred to was handed down in the seats of orthodox learning; and the Pali version of it, still preserved to us, has come from the great Buddhist seminary of the Mahā Vihāra in Ceylon. There is no reason why the supporters of the orthodox school should have modified or recast this tradition. There may have been mistakes, no doubt, but, in the absence of any motive to the contrary, there is no valid reason for refusing to accept the tradition as a bona-fide statement of what they held to be true.

Now this work and its commentary are so important for a history of the development of Buddhism that, although much pressed by other work which prevented my undertaking an edition of the text, I made a complete analysis, from a manuscript in my possession, of each of the questions raised in the Kathā Vatthu, and published it in 1892 in the *Journal of the Royal Asiatic Society*. It is impossible here to discuss the results in any detail, but two general conclusions may be stated with advantage.

In the first place, there had survived, at the time when the Kathā Vatthu was written (that is to say, in B. C. 250), only a small proportion of the seventeen schools, whose names have been handed down by tradition. Some of them only come before us in the pages of the Kathā Vatthu Commentary as the supporters of one or two theses of no very great importance.

But five of the schools are mentioned pretty frequently, and of these, the two principal are the Uttarā-pāṭhakas, or Northerners, and the Dakkhiṇa-pāṭhakas, or Southerners. This conclusion is entirely confirmed from two sources, which are mutually quite independent.

The one is the inscriptions. Among the ruins of the Buddhist topes, now being investigated by the Archeological Survey of India, are found a number of votive tablets on which are inscribed the names of the donors. For the most part these are personal names only, but quite occasionally the name of the school to which the person belonged is incidentally added. No doubt at the time when the tablets were put up there may have been two or more persons of the same name living in the locality, and the description is added for the sake of distinction. I have collected all the instances of this in my article, and the result agrees with the conclusions derived from the Kathā Vatthu and its Commentary.

The other confirmation comes from a source not so authoritative as being much later. But it is equally independent and more complete. Yuan Thsang, in the account of his travels in India, mentions, in regard to each locality, the estimated number of Buddhist recluses in each place at that time, *i. e.*, the early part of the seventh century. The list is a very long one, but I have thoroughly analysed it in an article in the *Journal of the Royal Asiatic Society* for 1892. The conclusions to be drawn from it as to the comparative prevalence of the various schools substantially coincide with the conclusions drawn from the Kathā Vatthu and its commentary.

The subject-matter of the differences in opinion between the orthodox and the other schools had, no doubt, in the time of Yuan Thsang assumed greater proportions. He gives no details, but it seems from the Kathā Vatthu that, in B. C. 250, the differences were principally of three kinds. In the first place we find that in the North and also in the South the old heresy of the soul-theory had crept back by side issues into the doctrine from which it had been categorically and explicitly excluded by Gotama and his earlier followers. In the second place we find that the exaltation of their revered Master had led some of his followers to go far beyond the belief in objective miraculous phenomena at his birth and at his death, and had produced a belief also in the personal superiority of their Master above the ordinary laws which govern human life. They not only believed that the earth was illumined at his birth, that flowers fell from heaven, that his mother's conception was immaculate, that he was transfigured before the eyes of his disciples, that an earthquake was occasioned by his birth and death, but that he himself was "*Lokuttara*" (above the common, superhuman, transcendental), not only in moments of supreme enlightenment, but in all the ordinary affairs of life. And thirdly, we find the germs of a belief we shall meet with farther on which proved even more disruptive in its tendency than either of the two we have mentioned—that is, that the real ideal for the Buddhist to aim at was, not Arahatship, the centre point and crown of the earlier Buddhism, but Bodhisatship, the essential doctrine of what is self-complacently called by its followers the Mahā Yāna, or Greater Vehicle.

All these three notions do in fact hang together, support one another, and have eventually developed into a system diametrically antagonistic to Gotama's own doctrine of a salvation in this life in Arahatship by self-culture and self-control. The materials are not yet available from which an accurate history of the fall can be drawn out in consecutive order, or in sufficiency of detail; and I do not envy the historian who shall take up the task of tracing the gradual intrusion of animistic and transcendental views, and beliefs in the supernatural, into the purely human and psychological ethics of the earlier system. But it is already possible to show the lines along which the later speculation went, and to trace the causes of the recrudescence of the errors which Gotama's reform was intended to kill.

You will recollect that there is included in the Buddhist canon a collection of the Indian folk-lore of that time, in which Gotama the Buddha himself in a previous birth has been identified with the hero of each particular story. The greatness and goodness and insight of the Buddha were in the eyes of his followers much too perfect to have been wrought out or developed in a single lifetime. Through ages upon ages he had gradually exercised himself in the *Pāramitās* (or sublime conditions), necessary to the attainment of Buddhahood. These are Generosity and Kindness and Renunciation and Wisdom and Resolution and Patience and Love of Truth and Energy and Good-will and Equanimity. At the end of each existence the Karma, that is, the doing or action accumulated in the previous birth, was handed on to a new individual who (though from the Christian point of view different from the others as having no continuing memory and no consciousness of identity) was, according to the Buddhist standpoint, the same individual, as being the product of the same Karma. And the Buddhist books glow with the fervour of gratitude in passages where they describe the self-abnegation of the Blessed One who submitted to be born again and again, that he might bring about the emancipation of mankind. For all through this time, whenever he was re-born as a man, he might, according to the view even of the orthodox school, have attained to Arahatship. The Karma which he inherited would no longer, then, have been re-individualised. It would have been dissipated in the good effect which his actions, his Karma, might have had upon other individuals. But that particular chain of existence would have been broken, the *Pāramitās* would never have been accomplished, and Gotama would not have become the Buddha. The Buddha therefore had, in his previous existences, deliberately abandoned that ideal which, in his historical existence, he urged men to set before them as their goal.

It is scarcely surprising, therefore, that the mistake began to be made of regarding the Bodhisat (that is, one of the individuals in the chain of those who were perfecting the *Pāramitās*) as a higher being than the Arahat. I say the mistake, for it was a mistake in two senses. The old Buddhist tradition rarely states that the Bodhisat was consciously pursuing the aim of becoming a Buddha. I only know of one passage older than the fifth century of our era in which this idea is put forward. And it was also a mistake from the ethical point of view. For from the moment that Arahatship began to be looked down upon in comparison with Bodhisatship, the whole system of mental training and self-control began to be neglected and even ignored.

The results of this took a long time to work out their full effect. One standard work of perhaps the principal of the seventeen schools—the Lokuttaravādins, or Transcendentalists—has survived. It is written in Sanskrit, and is being now edited, with a quite unusual degree both of care and of scholarship, by M. Émile Senart of Paris. The date of the work has not been ascertained with any certainty, but it is probably at least as old as the second century B.C. These Transcendentalists were the school which represented most nearly the views of those who held the Great Council; and so far as the edition has gone, it gives a very curious view of the position which they held. I have not noticed a single passage in which any of the propositions laid down in the Dialogues, is, in so many words, denied or even disputed; but the whole point of view has become entirely different, and it must have required a considerable time for so great a change to have taken place. Practically speaking the whole burden of the Dialogues is Arahatship, or one or other of the thirty-seven constituent elements of Arahatship. In the Mahā Vastu, which is the name of this manual of the Transcendentalists, Arahatship is indeed incidentally taken for granted as an ideal, if not *the* ideal. But the burden of the book is the consideration, from various points, of the stages which lead, not to Arahatship, but to Bodhisatship. It will be easier to speak more absolutely when M. Senart shall have finished his great work, but this is the impression which the volumes already published make upon the careful reader.

In the "Lotus of the Good Law" (the Saddharma Puṇḍarīka, as it is called in Sanskrit), of which we have a French translation by M. Burnouf, and a translation into English by Prof. Kern of Leiden, we find a stage far beyond that which has been reached in the Mahā Vastu of the Transcendentalists. In the Lotus we find that Arahatship is explicitly condemned, and Bodhisatship held up as the goal at which every good Buddhist has to aim; and the whole exposition of this theory, so subversive of the original Buddhism, is actually placed in the mouth of Gotama himself. The doctrine of Bodhisatship as the ideal is here called the Greater

Vehicle, as opposed to the Lesser Vehicle of Arahatship.

The Mahā Yāna doctors said, in effect: "We grant you all you say about the bliss of attaining Nirvana in this life. But it produces advantage chiefly to yourselves. And according to your own theory there will be a necessity for Buddhas in the future as much as there has been for Buddhas in the past. Greater, higher, nobler, then, than the attainment of Arahatship must be the attainment of Bodhisatship from a desire to save all living creatures in the ages that will come."

The new teaching therefore was in no conscious contradiction to the old. It accepted it all and was based upon it. Its distinguishing characteristic was the great stress which is laid on one point of the earlier doctrine to the gradual overshadowing of the rest. Its strength lay in the grandeur of its appeal to self-renunciation. It is true the newer school unconsciously thereby changed the centre point of the system, the focus of their mental vision. But it was at least no slight merit to have been led, even though they were led astray, by a sense of duty to the race. They might have been wiser, had they seen more clearly the originality of Gotama's system of ethics, and perceived that the race would really be benefited much more largely by the older doctrine of Arahatship, than by the new stress laid upon Bodhisatship. But readers of the Mahā Yāna books, tedious as these have so often been called, and rightly called, will find them acquire a new significance, and even a new beauty, when they are read in the light of this conception. The whole history of this development of belief, firstly in the putting of Arahatship into the background, and putting the Jātaka stories and the road of Bodhisatship into the foreground; and then the actual contempt of Arahatship, and the adoption, to its explicit as well as its virtual exclusion, of Bodhisatship, has yet to be written. The final step is attributed by later chroniclers, Tibetan and Chinese, to Nāgārjuna. And there are works extant, though only in Tibetan and Chinese translations, which are attributed to him. These works, however, are not yet accessible to the West; and of the Hīna Yāna books (that is to say, the books of the older schools which led on to the final result) we have only the Mahā Vastu, and the Sanskrit poems on the life of Buddha which were mentioned in my third lecture. But it is possible already to point out some of the results which followed from the newer doctrine. That the progress was very slow we know from the statements of Yuan Thsang. For in his time, that is, as late as the sixth century of our era, two thirds of the members of the Buddhist Order still adhered to the older doctrine. And in Nālandā, the great Buddhist university of that time, both the schools seem to have been represented.

As the Bodhisat theory loomed larger and larger before the minds of the Buddhists, their thoughts naturally turned with peculiar reverence to the Bodhisats of the past, the present, and the future, rather than to the Arahats whose names are recorded in the sacred books. Thus Nāgārjuna himself is looked upon by the Chinese as a Bodhisat, and Yuan Thsang mentions a number of persons, leaders in the newer school, with the title of Bodhisat. So the "Lotus of the Good Law" imitates the older Dialogues by giving a kind of introductory story describing the place and the occasion, on which Gotama is said to have propounded this much later work. And the persons to whom it is addressed, the assembly which surrounded him on that occasion, consists of a number of Bodhisats, instead of the actual persons by whom we know that the historical Buddha was in his lifetime surrounded. For not only were distinguished human beings singled out as Bodhisats, but a vast number of hypothetical beings were introduced as objects of reverence and worship on the ground that they were Bodhisats. As time went on, converts to this later Buddhism, who were well acquainted with the Hindu gods and goddesses of the day, thought to bring about a reconciliation between the two faiths by simply turning the Hindu gods and goddesses into Bodhisats, and representing them as supporters of the Buddha.

One of the chief agents in this line of development seems to have been Asanga, an influential monk of Peshawur in the Panjāb, who lived and wrote the first text-book of the creed—the Yogācāra Bhūmi Çāstra—about the sixth century of our era. He managed with great dexterity to reconcile the two opposing systems by placing a number of Saivite gods in the Pantheon of his newer Buddhism, and by incorporating into it a great deal of mystic Tantric doctrine from the prevalent animism. He thus made it possible for the half-converted, rude tribes to remain Buddhists while they brought offerings, and even bloody offerings, to these more congenial shrines; and while their practical beliefs had no relation at all to the four Truths or the Noble Eightfold Path, but busied itself almost wholly with attaining magic powers (Siddhi), by means of magic phrases (Dhārani) and magic circles (Maṇḍala). These Mahā Yāna books inculcating the new doctrines were translated, along with the older ones, into Chinese. Yuan Thsang regarded himself as a

Mahāyānist, took many books of the Greater Vehicle back to China, and in his labours as a translator was imitated by a long line of workers in the same field. The later books were afterwards translated into Tibetan, and the new doctrine attained in Tibet to so great a development, that Tibetan Buddhism, or rather Lamaism, has come to be the exact contrary of the earlier Buddhism. It has been worked up there into a regular system which has shut out all of the earlier Buddhism, although a few of the earlier books are also to be found in Tibetan translations.

In China, on the contrary, we find no evidence of a special system. All the books, early and late, are mixed together in one heterogeneous collection. Though no doubt the books of the Great Vehicle have by far the preponderating influence, yet books of various ages are still studied, and different schools in China have adopted different degrees of the newer doctrine.

Buddhism was introduced into Japan in the sixth century from the Korea, and having started there at so late a date, it has retained very little of the older doctrine, except the theories of impermanence, of the sorrow inherent in individuality, and of the absence of any abiding principle as set out in my fourth lecture. There are indeed now many sects of Buddhists in that country, but their divisions are entirely distinct from the divisions into Greater and Lesser Vehicle. All of them are founded on the Greater Vehicle, and they have developed in various ways along purely local lines. There are even members of the Order to be found there who are married clergy, and who preach a salvation to be reached in heaven.

But it is especially in Tibet that the doctrine of Bodhisatship has received its most curious development; and there alone is it, that the head of the Buddhist Order has also become the temporary ruler of the state, and is considered as being himself a living Bodhisat. In my *Hibbert Lectures* there will be found (pp. 192–195) a statement of the very curious and interesting similarities between this latest phase of the corruption of Buddhism, and the latest phase of Christianity in Rome.

In this connection I shall doubtless be expected to say a few words on Theosophy, if only because one of the books giving an account of that very curious and widely spread movement has been called *Esoteric Buddhism*. It has always been a point of wonder to me why the author should have chosen this particular title for his treatise. For if there is anything that can be said with absolute certainty about the book it is, that it is not esoteric,

14

and not Buddhism. The original Buddhism was the very contrary of esoteric. Gotama was accustomed, throughout his long career, to speak quite openly to everyone of the whole of the view of life which he had to propound. No doubt there were a certain number of questions to which it was his habit to refuse to reply. These were questions the discussion of which, in his opinion, was apt to lead the mind astray, and so far from being conducive to a growth in insight, would be a hindrance to the only thing which was supremely worth aiming at,—the perfect life in Arahatship. The reason for his reticence was not at all that he had formulated any doctrine upon them which he wished to conceal from some people, and reveal only to other more intimate disciples. Such questions as—What shall I be during the ages of the future? Do I after all exist, or am I not? How am I? This is a being: Whence did it come? And whither will it go?—are regarded as worse than unprofitable, and the Buddha not only refused to discuss them, but held that the tendency, the desire to discuss them was a weakness, and that the answers usually given were a delusion. There are a whole set of such questions, drawn up in identical words in several of the Dialogues, a consideration of which is called the Walking in Delusion, the Jungle, the Wilderness, the Puppet Show, the

Writhing, the Fetter of Delusion. Gotama says, just before he dies, in a passage I have already read to you: "I have preached the truth without making any distinction between exoteric and esoteric doctrine; for in respect of the truths, Ānanda, the Tathāgata has no such thing as the closed fist of a teacher who keeps some things back." And it is quite impossible for anyone who reads the Pali books to avoid seeing that everything which the Master himself, and his early disciples, regarded as important is not only set out with a lavish exposition which seeks above all to make the whole matter clear to everybody, but is even explained with a length of detail which those not interested in the system find tedious in the extreme. There is not the slightest hint throughout the whole of the Piṭakas of any esoteric teaching. And even as late as the *Milinda* we find the ideal teacher described in the following words: "He should be zealous, teach nothing partially, keep nothing secret, and hold nothing back."* It is only when the Mahā Yāna books, written many centuries after the time of Gotama, wished to father on the Buddha opinions different from those which he actually promulgated, that we find the allegation, in Buddhist

* *Questions of King Milinda*, vol. i., p. 142 of my translation. Compare also the note at pp. 267, 268.

books, of an esoteric teaching. It was the only way in which the writers of those books could at the same time call themselves Buddhist followers of Gotama, and yet put forward the new ideas, contrary to those of Gotama, which they were anxious to propagate.

And not only was there nothing esoteric in the real original Buddhism. The views expressed in *Esoteric Buddhism*, so far as they are Indian at all, are not esoteric. The study of self-induced trance is common to all the Indian schools. All that is taught on the subject is accessible in handbooks, and the teachers who practised themselves in such things are always willing to teach them to anyone who will submit to the necessary discipline. In this sense only is it that Indian teachers, other than the Buddhist, can occasionally be described as esoteric. And this is a sense in which the word is also applicable to our own teachers in the universities of the West. They will not admit to their classes any chance comer who has not undergone the necessary discipline to enable him to appreciate what they have to say. All the talk about "astral body" and the different kinds of "soul," seven more or less, which is, or rather was, put forward as esoteric Buddhism, is a part of the Yoga philosophy of India, which is perfectly accessible to all the world.

And so far as I have been able to ascertain (though the later Buddhists were much given to magic and Tantric charms), this happens to be a part of the current Indian belief on those subjects which even they have never adopted. It is of course diametrically opposed to all the most essential Buddhist doctrines as set out in outline in my last two lectures. You will see therefore, why I venture to say that the views put forward, in the work referred to, are neither esoteric, nor are they Buddhism.

At the same time it is fair to add that Theosophists in general do not any longer, I believe, describe their tenets under the name of Esoteric Buddhism, and we must not forget that there are Theosophists and Theosophists. There are not a few among them who are doing good service in helping to break down that ignorant self-complacency which regards any notions differing from the current notions held in the West as quite unworthy of notice. There are not a few of them who have really devoted themselves to a patient study of Eastern philosophies and Eastern religions, and who have rendered real service to scholarship by bringing over MSS. and providing funds for the publication of translations of Eastern books. There may be much in Theosophy which suggests a superficial curiosity into obscure questions of psycho-physics, and into half-savage practices of magic, black and white. But no one can doubt the sincerity of such Theosophists as those to whom I have just referred. I regret that an unfortunate title, now no longer emphasised by Theosophists themselves, should have led very widely to a confusion between a great and sane system of philosophical ethics, and speculations of very doubtful validity (really in many instances, the rebound of half-trained intellects from a crass materialism) and mixed up with historical heresies of a most startling character.

It is very instructive to notice the fact that the name of Buddhism has been rejected by the leading expounders of Theosophy. This fact is really an unconscious tribute to the success of the efforts that have been made in the last few years to render the authorities of the real, original Buddhism accessible to the Western world. And I venture to think that the publication and translation of the Buddhist texts may possibly have no little influence among the more cultured of those Eastern peoples, who still call themselves Buddhists although they have wandered, in many respects, so far from the ancient faith. When Japanese students, for instance, come to our Western colleges and learn there to read their Pali and Sanskrit books under the guidance of professors trained in historical criticism, it is almost impossible that they can return to their own country without the accuracy of their knowledge being greatly improved, and their ideas of Buddhism, to some extent at least, corrected and modified. We have an admirable instance of this in the very valuable catalogue of Chinese Sanskrit books published by Mr. Bunyiu Nanjio, at the University Press of Oxford. Prepared under the guidance of the distinguished Professor of Comparative Philology at Oxford, Professor Max Müller, this book is a model of what such a catalogue ought to be, with discussions about dates, and careful indexes to all the names of the books and authors mentioned. Mr. Bunyiu Nanjio, while in London and Oxford, studied Buddhist Sanskrit, and has now returned to Japan to occupy the post of Professor at the University of Tokio.

This is one of the excellent results following on the increased intercommunication between East and West which are now becoming so frequent, and which we owe to the victories over nature achieved by Western science. It was the desire of peoples to travel and have intercourse with one another which was one of the principal means of spurring on inventions. And the inventions, in their turn, have made possible such a meeting as the Parliament of Religions at Chicago, where minds steeped exclusively in Western and New-World ideas listened, not only with interest, but also with sympathy, greatly heightened by the presence of their representatives, to the expositions of Eastern creeds.

It is true that a perusal of the numerous speeches made at that Congress (and I have read the Buddhist ones very carefully) show how astounding is the gulf on all sides between popular beliefs and the conclusions of scholarship. To take only one instance from the address on Buddha by the Right Rev. Zitsuzen Ashitsu of Japan. He says: "The Person of Buddha is perfectly free from life and death. We call it *Nehan* or *Nirvana*. *Nehan* is divided into four classes: (1) The name given to the nature of Buddha which has neither beginning nor end and is entirely clear of lust like a perfect mirror. But such an excellent nature as I have mentioned is not the peculiar property of Buddha, but every being in the world has just the same constitution. (2) The name given to the state, little advanced from the above, where we perceive that our solicitude is fleeting, our lives are inconstant, and even that there is no such thing as Ego. In this state our mind is quite empty and clear, but there still remains one thing, the body. So it is called *Uyo*, or something left. (3) The state in which our body and intellect come to entire annihilation and there is nothing traceable, therefore this state is called *Muyo*, or nothing left. (4) The state when we get perfect intellectual wisdom. We are not any more subject to birth and death. Also we become perfectly merciful; we are not content with the indulging state of highest Nirvana; but we appear to the beings of every class to save them from prevailing pains by imparting the pleasure of Nirvana. Out of these four classes of Nirvana the first and last are called the Nirvana of Mahayana, the Greater Vehicle, while the remainder are that of Hīna Yāna, the Lesser Vehicle."

We must of course take into consideration, in this quotation, the imperfection of the English. But the curious thing about it is that the views here ascribed to the Hīna Yāna, can not be found, so far as we know, in any Hīna Yāna book. And this difficulty does not seem to have occurred to the learned author, who also distinctly states that the Mahā Yāna books (really many centuries later) were compiled by the disciples of the Buddha, meaning no doubt his personal followers. It will be very interesting to be able to trace how these notions passed through the intermediate stages between the doctrine of the Piṭakas and the doctrine here set forth. I have not time now to discuss the resemblances and differences which are involved, but it will be apparent to you all how different is the tone of the passage I have just quoted from the passages I have had occasion to read from the Buddhist Piṭakas themselves.

Another excellent result which may, and I hope will, follow from our increased acquaintance with the actual thoughts and literature, as well as with the personalities of Oriental peoples, is a loosening of that prejudice which undoubtedly obtains, even among scholarly circles, in the West. It would be perhaps too much to complain that classical scholars, for instance, should have a decided repugnance to admit any actual influence on Greek thought or institutions as having been exercised by the thinkers of the East, however ungrudgingly that privilege is conceded to Egypt. Personally I think that they are quite in the right in maintaining that such an influence is, except in a few instances, at present entirely unproven. But surely there are many points of analogy which are most instructive, and suggestive at least of more than an analogical connection; points that may throw light upon the natural course of the evolution of human conceptions and, in doing so, help to throw light on dark corners of the history of that culture out of which our own has arisen. It is a common saying that it is impossible to know any one language well without at the same time knowing another, and I venture to think that a similar remark holds good of the history of religion or of ethics, or of institutions, or of philosophy.

Should I be considered too bold if I were to go one step farther and suggest that there are really some points in the philosophy of the East, and especially of India, which are fated sooner or later to find their place in, and to exercise a not inconsiderable influence over, the thought of Western nations. I know it is a common idea, and one held not only by Philistines, that the study of Buddhism, for instance, is of no use except as a matter of curiosity, since it has no connection with the origins of our own culture, which is, after all, in the commonly accepted opinion, the only progressive culture in the world. This view not only entirely ignores the value of the comparative study of all historical questions, but it ignores also, with an almost wilful ignorance, the real originality of Gotama's ethics and philosophy.

But this, I know, is not the view which is held by those I have the honour of addressing, or indeed by some of the most unprejudiced and original leaders of thought in Europe. You all know how Schopenhauer claims to have arrived, in the very deepest foundation of his system, at a practical agreement with Buddhism, and he writes, alluding to other thinkers:

"If I am to take the results of my philosophy as the standard of truth, I should be obliged to concede to Buddhism the pre-eminence over the rest. In any case it must be a satisfaction to me to find my teaching in such close agreement with a religion professed by the majority of men. This agreement must be all the more satisfactory because in my philosophising I have certainly not been under its influence."

These words are at least conclusive evidence to show that, so far as Schopenhauer is worth studying, the Buddhist philosophy is worthy of study also; and I need not stay therefore to point out the reasons which have led me to believe that Schopenhauer *was* influenced, not only by Vedantism, but also by Buddhism.

And with this great philosophical thinker I would also remind you of the words of the veteran leader of scientific thought in England, Professor Huxley, who, comparing Gotama's idealism with that of Bishop Berkeley, says, in one of his latest utterances:

"It is a remarkable indication of the subtlety of Indian speculation that Gotama should have seen deeper than the greatest of modern idealists."

And throughout his whole essay he insists very strongly on the value, even to actual belief in the West, of a critical study of the Buddhist system.

Dr. Deussen, Professor of Philosophy at Kiel, has even gone so far as to publish a handbook for students entitled *Elements of Metaphysics*, in which Indian thought is throughout compared and used, alongside with European speculation. And I know from your presence here to-day, that you at least will cordially agree with the committee representing centres of higher education in America, that the comparative study of religious belief (which must be very largely, and even mainly, the history of Oriental belief) has come to be a matter of real importance to Western students. It would be beyond the scope of a lecturer on this subject to touch upon the possible influence of its study upon the religion of the future. But it is a matter of historic fact that the great epochs of intellectual progress have been precisely those when two different and even antagonistic systems of thought have been fermenting in the same minds. The two systems are, as it were, the father and mother, whose progeny, more like, perhaps, to one of its parents, still possesses some of the characteristics of both, and escapes from the evil results of too exclusive and narrow an interbreeding.

We may at least venture to hope that the series of lectures, of which this course is only the first instalment, will do much to promote that feeling of respect for opinions we ourselves can never hold, which lends so much assistance to a right understanding of the causes at work in the evolution of thought and in the history of our race.

THE END.

INDEX.

Abhidhamma, 62
Abhidhāna Padīpikā, 49
Acchariya Abbhuta Sutta, 95
Ajanta, cave hermitages, 118
Ālāra Kālāma, 102
Anatta Lakkhaṇa Sutta, 39
Anguttara, 60, 61
Animism, 36, 140
Arahatship, 145, 148, 149, 155; defined, 150, 164; poems on, 166 foll.
Arbitration, 56.
Ariya Pariyesana Sutta, 102
Arnold, Matthew, 183
Arnold, Sir Edwin, 89
Aryan religion, 185
Aryans, 16–18
Ascetics, 96–99; the five, 103–106
Asoka, 15, 46, 64
Aspiration, its importance, 137, 182
Atheists, 13

Bastian, Prof., 155
Beal, the Rev. Samuel, 91
Bhagavad Gītā, 141
Bigandet, Bishop, 87
Bode, Mrs., 74
Bodhisatship, 201–203
Brahma Vihāra, 148

Brahmins, their treatment of Buddhism, 115, 116
"Buddha Carita," the poem, 88
Buddhaghosa, the great commentator, 28, 62, 108
"Buddha Vansa," poem on the Buddhas, 77

Carpenter, Mr. J. E., 28
Cause, universality of, 32, 42
Cave dwellings, ancient Buddhist, 118, 119
Ceremonies, evil of, 147
Ceylon books, 46
Chalmers, Mr. Robert, 79, 95
Chicago Parliament of Religions, 215, 216
Childers, Prof., 49
Chinese Buddhism, 8
Cicero, 1, 4
Conduct, the right, 137
Confections, 130, 156
Council, of Vesāli, 190–194; the Great, 193, 202
Cowell, Prof., 79, 88

Dakkhiṇa-pāṭhakas, the, 197
Delusion of self, 126–129, 131, 141, 142
Desires, *see* Aspiration.
Deussen, Prof., 25, 221
Development of Buddhist doctrine, 189, 196
Devils, formerly gods, 12, 14
Dhammapada, 48, 68
Dhammapāla, the commentator, 71
Dhamma Sangaṇi, 63
Dhaniya Sutta, translated, 166
Dharma = Dhamma, 2, 38, 41, 63, 106, 145
Dialogues of the Buddha, 58, 59, 156, 189, 195, 203
Dīgha Nikāya, 27, 28, 30
Dīpa Vansa, quoted, 193
Doubt, the fetter of, 142–145
Dreams, 10, 11
Drink, 148
Dualism, 37

"Ecce Homo," 4
Education, early methods of, 19, 58
Effort, the right, 137
Elephanta cave hermitages, 118
Emancipation, 183, 184
Empedokles, 161
Equanimity, 149
Esoteric teaching, none in Buddhism, 209, 211
Evil, origin of, 125
Evils, the four great, 141, 178
Evolution, of religious belief, 140; of ethical character, 162

Faith and works, 146, 176
Fate, mystery of, 130, 157
Fausböll, Prof., 48
Fetters, the Ten, 141 foll.
Final assurance, Buddhist doctrine of, 147
Finity and infinity, 31
Foucaux, Prof., 88
Foundation of the Kingdom of Righteousness, 106, 135-140
Freedom, Buddhist, 184
Future life, 32; poems on, 77; in Buddhism, 128, 131, 132, 134; one of the four great evils, 141; love of, is one of the fetters, 150; the Arahat untarnished by love of, 177

Garbe, Prof., 25, 162
God, 21; eternity of, 31
Gods, the earliest, 11; eternity of, 31

Harrison, Frederic, 4
Heaven, not to be desired, 131, 150; Buddhist idea of, not the Christian, 154
Heresies, the, 27, 31 foll., 62; at the Council of Vesāli, 190-192
Huxley, Prof., 220

Ignorance, 126, 141; the last fetter, 150; in the Wheel of Life, 155, 165
Ill-will, the fifth fetter, 148

Impermanence, Indian doctrine of, 121 foll., 129
Individuality, the cause of sorrow, 124, 142; not denied in Buddhism, 125; the delusions regarding it, 126, 127, 131
Indulgences, the ten, 191
Intelligence, result of, 141
"Iti Vuttaka," book so called, 70, 71

Jacobi, Prof., 24
Japanese Buddhism, 208, 215
Jātakas, old stories, 78
Jewels, the seven, of the Blessed One, 184
Jina Carita, poem on Buddha's life, 88

Kapila, founder of the Sānkhya, 24, 26, 29
Karma, theory of, 129 foll., 133, 170, 200
Kassapa of Uruvelá, 166
Kathā Vatthu, 40, 63, 195 foll.
Kern, Prof., 203
Khandakas, 56
Khuddaka Pāṭha, 67
Konfucius, 8, 140

"Lalita Vistara," poem, 88, 89
Lanman, Prof., 76
Lao Tsü, 8
Law, ancient meaning of 2; early discussion of points of, 55, 58
Liberty of thought, 115, 116, 184
"Light of Asia," the poem, 89, 104, 158
Livelihood, right means of, 137
Lotus of the good law, 203
Love, Buddhist exercise of, 149, 174, 176
Lupton, Mr., 98

Mahā Pajāpatī, the Buddha's aunt, 93
Mahā Parinibbāna Sutta, 113, 143, 179
Mahā Vastu, 202–204
Māra, the Evil One, 73, 75, 104
Materialists, Indian, 24, 37

Māyā, the Buddha's mother, 93
Medicine, 400 B.C., 57, 179
Memory, 19, 34
Milinda, 40, 171, 184
Mindfulness, the right, 137
Monistic theories, 23
Monotheism, 21, 140
Morality, mere, not enough, 147
Müller, Prof. Edward, 63, 72
Müller, Prof. Max, 5

Nāgārjuna, 206
Nāgasena, 40, 171
Name, part of personality, 157
Niddesa, an ancient commentary, 76
Nirvana, referred to, 135, 145 ; defined, 150, 164 ; poems on, 167 foll. ; realisation of, 172–175 ; place of, 175
Noble Condition, 148
Noble Eightfold Path, 135–137
Noble Truths, the four, 138

Pabbajjā Sutta, translated, 99 foll.
Pahlavi Texts, 141
Pāli, 45 foll., 81
Pāli Text Society, 81–86
Pantheism, 36
Pāramitās, the ten, 200
Parivāra, 58
Path, the noble eightfold, 135–137
Pātimokkha, 54, 57
Pavāranā, 56
Penance, 102
Peta-Vatthu, 77
Pindar, 161
Piṭakas, 51–53, 81, 195
Pity, practice of, 149
Piyadassi, 46
Plato, 59, 159, 161, 163
Polytheism, 36, 140

Potter and his wheel, 156, 157
Predestination, 130
Pride, last enemy to be conquered, 150
Primitive man, 9
Primordial stuff, 28
Prinsep, 46
Puggala Paññatti, 63
Pythagoras, 162

Rāhula, the Buddha's son, 93
Rāma, Uddaka's father, 102
Rapture, the right, 137, 146, 152, 177
Raṭṭhapāla Suttanta, 98
Recluse, the Buddhist, described, 176 foll.
Religion, defined, 1–5 ; in India, 6–9
Renunciation, 96, 97
Rhys Davids, Mrs., 63, 72, 183
Rouse, Mr. W. H. D., 79
Rules of the Order, 53–58 ; 190–192

Salvation, what it is, 131, 154
Samyutta, 61
Sānkhya philosophy, 24 foll.
Scaliger, 44
Schelling, Prof., 131
Schism, the first, 190
Schopenhauer, 219, 220
Schurman, President, 186
Self, delusions of, *see* Delusion.
Self-reliance, essential in Buddhism, 143, 176, 180
Self-righteousness, the ninth fetter, 150
Senart, M. Emile, 202
Sense-perception, 158
Sensuality, one of the four great evils, 141, 147
Sisters of the Order, 56
Sorrow, cause of, 124, 125
Soul, early belief in, 10 ; eternity of the, 31 ; Buddhist doctrine about, 39–41 ; belief in a, fatal to goodness, 123, 124 ; not the real link between this life and the next, 128, 133

Speech, the right, 137
Stoics, why like the Buddhists, 140
St. Thomas Aquinas, 2
Sutta, 53
Sutta Nīpāta, poems so-called, 76
Sutta Vibhanga, 55
Symonds, Mr. J. A., 152
Sympathy, 149

Tanhā, *see* Thirst.
Taylor, Mr. Arnold C., 62, 65
Temperance, Buddhist, 148, 152
Tevijja Sutta, 164
Theosophy, 209–212
Thera-therī-gāthā, Songs of the Elders, 71
Thirst, 136, 158
Thought, the method of its growth, 13
Tissa, author of Kathā Vatthu, 63, 195
Toleration, in India, 115 ; among the Buddhists, 116, 184
Transcendentalists, 199, 202
Transmigration, 128–131, 154. 183
Trench, Archbishop, 3
Truth, *see* Dhamma.
Truths, the four noble, 136
Turnour, George, 46, 47

Udāna, Ecstatic utterance, 70
Uddaka, son of Rāma, 102
Upādāna, grasping, 158, 164
Uposatha, 54, 56
Uttará-pāṭhakas, the Northerners, 197

Vedāntism, 22, 24
Vedas, show an advanced stage in the soul theory, 13, 14
Vehicles, the Greater and the Less, 204
Vesālī, Council of, 191
Views, the right, 137
Vimāna Vatthu, the poem, 77

Vinaya, Canon Law, 53-58
von Schroeder, Prof., 162

Waddell, Mr., 119, 156
Wandering ascetics, 96-99
Warren, Mr. H. C., 160, 176
West, Mr., 141
Wheel of Life, 120, 155 foll., 161
Whirlpool of rebirths, 155
Women, made the earliest gods, 11; teachers and poets in early Buddhism, 72-75
Works and faith, 146, 147

Yuan Thsang, 205, 207